The SWEET SIDE of SOURDOUGH

50 Irresistible Recipes for Pastries, Buns,
Cakes, Cookies and More

The SWEET SIDE
of SOURDOUGH

Caroline Schiff, Creator of Pastry Schiff

PAGE STREET
PUBLISHING CO.

PAGE STREET
PUBLISHING CO.

First published in 2021 by
Page Street Publishing Co.
27 Congress Street, Suite 105
Salem, MA 01970
www.pagestreetpublishing.com

Distributed by Macmillan, sales in Canada by The Canadian Manda Group.

25   24   23   22   21   1   2   3   4   5

ISBN-13: 978-1-64567-422-1

ISBN-10: 1-64567-422-3

Library of Congress Control Number: 2021931371

Cover and book design by Kylie Alexander for Page Street Publishing Co.

Photography by Jonathan Meter

Printed and bound in the United States

DEDICATION

This book is dedicated to my family, who has unconditionally supported my baking ambitions from day one. To my mom, Robin Schiff, and brother, George Anesi, this book would not exist without your relentless love and encouragement. We are lucky people.

TABLE of CONTENTS

Introduction

Sourdough and I were frenemies for a long time. I tiptoed around it for years, because as a pastry chef, I figured it wasn't my thing. I stayed in my sweet lane: cakes, cookies, pies, ice cream, enriched doughs—but never sourdough bread. That was for the bakers. But inevitably, like so many of us, once I got into it, I got *into* it. Personally, and professionally, I've become obsessed with feeding, nurturing and baking with this incredible active fermentation. Sourdough is magic. I'm so smitten with this living thing that thrives on the air around it and lives off a unique microbiome and whatever natural yeasts it can gobble up but also needs my care and attention. A well-looked after sourdough starter will produce beautiful baked goods with a distinct personality from nothing more than grains, water and time. So, yeah: magic.

While I had gotten my hands into sourdough as the pastry chef at Gage & Tollner, it wasn't until the spring of 2020 that I really jumped on the so-called "trend." (It's like a zillion years old—it's not a trend.) Looking back, I realize my broken heart was slightly patched up during those uncertain days—seeing home bakers across the country take a stab at fermenting their own starters for the first time, sharing their bakes on Instagram, and finding solace, comfort and success in the oldest leavening technique we know. In those early weeks of lockdown, when my role changed from pastry chef to extremely overqualified home baker, I fermented an endless parade of loaves, having tasked myself with fostering our restaurant's sourdough starter at home. How could I let it perish? The daily feeding, stretching and folding became a kind of therapy that gave me some purpose, and I'd soothe my anxiety by shaping boules or dimpling focaccia on repeat, as the world outside became more uncertain by the day.

But even in a global pandemic, I have my loaf limits before overload sets in. After the first few weeks I felt the fatigue. I'd open my tiny, chaotic freezer and get pummeled by bags of presliced toast, while containers of croutons and deli pints of herbed breadcrumbs fell to the floor, bruising my big toe significantly along the way. I noticed others were dealing with the same situation. Bread burnout is real. Friends were texting, asking what else could they do with their starter. How can they use their discard? Can they make more than just bread? I wasn't sure, but my DMs on Instagram quickly filled up with inquiries, and this got my pastry chef brain going. What would a whole world of sweet sourdough applications look— and taste—like?

I began experimenting and started to regard my sourdough starter as a versatile ingredient that would enhance sweet recipes. I noticed mouthwatering tangy flavors, crunchier-than-ever streusels and impossibly crispy crusts with beautifully browned edges on my bakes. There was a certain *je ne sais quoi* to each bite of brownie, a holy grail texture to my classic chocolate chip cookie, complex flavors and satisfying texture juxtapositions abound. The copious amounts of discard became a reliable underdog, serving as the thickener for custards or finding a home in crêpes, crusts, crumbles and toppings. Pleasantly sweet and sour babkas, fluffy chocolate scones, tangy pie crusts loaded with fruit, focaccias drizzled generously with honey, just-sweet-enough cakes perfect for snacking, cookies with the perfect chew and just about everything in the pancake family. For all that I felt I had lost in the pandemic, I felt revived by these recipes. Sourdough kept my pastry brain engaged and fed my creative soul when it was hungriest.

The Sweet Side of Sourdough is about baking from the heart when I needed to the most. It's a story of comfort, creativity and inspiration during one of the most devastating events of our time and the personal resilience I found through this resourceful approach to sweets. These recipes were my lifeline; they were a way to nourish myself, friends, family and neighbors during a pandemic—and honestly, writing this book kept me going on my darkest of days. It often got me out of bed. This is a story about finding sweetness in the most unexpected places, so I hope you'll find some sweetness in these pages too.

ABOUT THE RECIPES

I want to give you a whole new way to look at your sourdough starter and an understanding of what it's capable of. This book will cover the basics of building and nurturing a simple starter from scratch followed by recipes using both active sourdough starter and occasionally the discard where it makes sense. The recipes range from complex 24-hour fermented loaves and enriched breads with levain builds (page 17) to snappy cakes you can make with an idle hour or two. Many can be executed simply, with no more than a mixing bowl and common utensils, most of which I bet you already have in your kitchen.

The Sweet Side of Sourdough is for everyone. It's beginner friendly and can kick off your sourdough adventure. The moderately challenging recipes are always approachable, making this the perfect book for when you've been baking loaves successfully and are ready to see what else your starter can do!

Caroline Schiff

Making a Starter and Building a Levain

I'll start this section off by saying that many first-timers find the idea of building and maintaining a sourdough starter confusing and intimidating. If that's you, I hear you, I see you and you're not alone. Sourdough has been around for thousands of years, and you can imagine that in that time, folks have discovered many approaches, theories and techniques. The more you read, the more your head might spin if you're just embarking on your sourdough journey, because there's just so much knowledge out there. This approach is what I learned from another chef—it made sense to me, and it worked for me, so I kept it up and built on it.

In the most basic terms, sourdough starter is a living culture: a mixture of fermented flour, water and microbes that feed on the natural yeasts in its environment. Wild yeast is everywhere—from the air to our skin. When it mixes with flour, the combination creates fermentation and gases that, when well-fed and active, have the power to make baked goods rise and taste amazingly complex. In building and maintaining a healthy, effective starter, it's good to remember a few key things.

First, flour quality. Use flours that are minimally processed and unbleached for the best flavor and activity. I like to kick off a new starter with a combination of rye and whole wheat flour, and then gradually introduce all-purpose flour as it becomes mature and active. The rye and whole wheat flours have a more robust microbiome and more natural yeasts than all-purpose flour, and I find that helps a new starter get going and mature faster. This blend also gives the starter a wonderful flavor. Once it has a healthy community of bacteria, I incorporate some all-purpose flour with each feeding, eventually settling into a balance of the three. The all-purpose flour lightens it up a bit and makes it a little more versatile for sweet applications. Once you get to know your starter and become comfortable with the routine, you can always feed it a little more or less of something to get the balance you're looking for in your baked goods.

Second, water temperature. I recommend feeding with water that hovers right above room temperature—in the 70°F (21°C) ballpark. You can use a thermometer, which many sourdough enthusiasts do, but once comfortable, you can do it by feel and get great results.

The building method I use is common—and I'll bet you've come across it before. It takes 6 to 14 days for sourdough starter to become mature enough to bake with. The good news is, once you've cultivated a mature starter, if looked after, you'll never have to do it again. Even if you take several weeks off from baking, there are lots of preservation methods out there that will keep your starter dormant until you're ready to wake it up and bake again. I typically keep mine in the fridge to "hibernate" until I want to bake again. It usually bounces back to life after two to three refreshing feedings. My great aunt Muriel has famously maintained the same starter since the 1970s. She calls him Carl, he lives in Flushing, Queens, and over the years he's been put into various states of hibernation and dormancy, always to successfully bounce back to life when needed.

This is a 100% hydration starter. Don't let the talk of hydration and percentages scare you. All it means is that the starter is comprised of equal parts flour and water and will always need the same ratio no matter how much you scale it up or down. For example, if you have 100 grams of starter, feed it 100 grams water and 100 grams flour. 1:1:1. A 100% hydration starter is, in my opinion, the most versatile and easy to maintain, so it's a nice jumping off point and what all the recipes in this book are based on. I like to keep 300 to 600 grams of starter on hand since I bake a lot. You can always scale up or down if your starter gets that same 1:1:1 ratio.

There's A LOT of information out there on temperature, ideal environments, feeding schedules, etc. You can read for hours on end and keep learning until you die if you want. The wealth of information is incredible but can also be overwhelming. I encourage you to read as much as you can on sourdough and learn from a diverse group of experts. Just keep in mind that when you find a method that works for you and makes sense, you're off to a great start (pun intended). My best advice? Don't overthink it.

Building a starter from scratch isn't difficult, but it takes time, so don't be discouraged if a week into the process you haven't seen progress yet. Everything from the ambient room temperature to the kinds of flours you use will affect its development. It can take up to 14 days, but typically you'll see some action by day 5 and can possibly even bake as soon as day 6. If at the end of this cycle your starter isn't growing yet, don't stress. Just keep it up for a few more days and keep an eye on it. It'll get there.

But how do I know my starter is healthy, mature and ready to use?!

Great question. There are a few sensory clues that will tell you when your starter is mature and ready to get to work! Visually, if you see your starter rising and then falling after being fed, typically over the course of 8 to 12 hours, that's a great indication that it's active enough to bake with. I like to use a piece of tape or rubber band to mark its starting point and track its growth after each feeding. When I see it has doubled in volume, I know it's ready.

The "float test" is another great way to see if your starter is ready to get to work. Once it's been fed and grows significantly—ideally when doubled in volume—drop no more than a tablespoon's worth into a glass of room-temperature water. If it floats on the surface, it means it's gassed up and good to go. If it sinks, it either needs more time or it's past its prime for that feeding. In terms of smell, you might notice a range of aromas from fruity to pleasantly boozy and yeasty, like beer or wine. That's also a great indicator of a healthy starter.

ESSENTIAL SUPPLIES

Before you embark on building your starter, make sure you have the essential tools and ingredients on hand.

Digital Scale

This is nonnegotiable. If you've been holding off on getting a digital scale and baking in grams, now is the time to rip the band-aid off. So, go get a scale and come back. I'll wait. . . . OK, great. Baking, and especially baking with sourdough, is one of those things where you'll get much more consistent results by weighing all the ingredients. And some recipes just won't work well if you don't scale them. Lots of the breads in this book fall into that category, so please try to use a scale for best results. You'll be much happier and make me happy too. Once you make the change to weighing your ingredients, you'll realize how much easier it is than pulling out a set of measuring cups, and you'll have fewer dishes to wash. A win-win situation, if you ask me.

Clear Glass or Plastic Vessel

Use a 1-quart (1-L) or larger glass jar with a lid or a plastic deli quart container with a lid. It should be clear so you can see what your starter is up to, and always provide enough room for the starter to double in volume. I use a variety of containers—from 16 ounces (480 ml) up to 1 gallon (3.8 L) in capacity—and alternate between them based on how much starter I'm maintaining.

A Rubber Band or Some Masking Tape

Any old kind will do! Just something to mark the growth of your starter as you feed it each day. Simply place the rubber band or a piece of tape around your container, exactly at the top line of the starter right after feeding. Check back periodically, and you'll see the level creep up as the fermentation gets going and gases build up!

Essential Flours

I keep a variety of high-quality flours on hand for feeding my starter, but I tend to bake almost exclusively with all-purpose flour for these recipes, adding rye or whole wheat here and there for flavor. If you can find fresh farmer-milled flours for your starter, especially when it comes to rye and whole wheat, even better. Check your local farmers' market or order directly from a mill. For all-purpose and bread flour, I swear by King Arthur. It's readily available and of great quality.

HOW TO BUILD YOUR SOURDOUGH STARTER

You can get going with sourdough baking right away by getting a little mature starter from a friend, but I encourage everyone to build a starter from scratch at least once. It's such a satisfying process, and it will deepen your understanding and appreciation for the art. Plus, it's just so cool to watch something ferment!

Day 1: In a clear 32-ounce (960-ml) vessel, combine 100 grams of water at about 70°F (21°C) with 50 grams of whole wheat flour and 50 grams of rye flour. Mix until no dry patches remain, cover with a secure lid and leave in a warm spot for 24 hours.

Day 2: Discard 100 grams of the mixture. To the remaining 100 grams of the mixture, add 100 grams of water at about 70°F (21°C) with 50 grams of whole wheat flour and 50 grams of rye flour. Mix until no dry patches remain, cover and leave in a warm spot for 24 hours. By the end of the day, you might see a few little bubbles and some growth, or you might not. Keep going!

Days 3 and 4: Discard all but 100 grams of the mixture. Add 100 grams of water at about 70°F (21°C) with 50 grams of whole wheat flour and 50 grams of rye flour. Mix until no dry patches remain, cover and leave in a warm spot for 24 hours, marking the starting level of the mixture with a rubber band or piece of tape so you can watch its growth, which will peak and fall over the 24-hour period. At this point you might see some action and you should smell a funky, fermented aroma that might be like super ripe fruit, wine or beer.

Day 5: Discard all but 100 grams of the mixture. Add 100 grams of water at about 70°F (21°C) with 25 grams of whole wheat flour, 25 grams of rye flour and 50 grams of all-purpose flour. Mix until no dry patches remain, cover and leave in a warm spot for 24 hours. This is the first day your starter is eating some all-purpose flour. Exciting!

Day 6: Today you'll bulk up the starter, so you'll want to find a slightly larger vessel. Your starter should be ready to bake with shortly! Discard all but 200 grams of the mixture. Add 200 grams of water at about 70°F (21°C) with 30 grams of whole wheat flour, 20 grams of rye flour and 150 grams of all-purpose flour. Mix until no dry patches remain, cover and leave in a warm spot. At this point your starter is likely ready to use and you have 600 grams to play with. If it's doubling in size from 4 to 8 hours after feedings and passes the float test, you're good to go! If not, give it another few days. Just follow this day 6 feeding routine each day around the same time, if you can manage it, to maintain your starter.

If you're not going to bake for a bit, you can transfer your starter to the fridge to hibernate. Two days before you want to bake, bring it up to room temperature and resume the day 6 feeding routine to "wake it up." I find mine usually comes back to its perky self after about two feedings.

What about the discard? I love using the discard, and there are several recipes in this book that allow you to use it in crêpes, blintzes, various streusel toppings and more. If it's a big day of baking, you might feed the entire starter to bulk it up and not have any discard at all—so it will fluctuate. If you're using discard in a recipe, try to use it at no more than 3 days old. Otherwise, I find it can be a little boozy and off-putting. Also note that discard weighs a not-insignificant amount more than fed, active starter, which is full of gas. Your best bet is to go by the gram amounts, but as an example, one cup of active starter weighs about 80% as much as discard, so remember that if you make any swaps. This conversion table is helpful:

Active to Discard Starter Conversions							
	1 cup	1 tsp	1 tbsp	¼ cup	⅓ cup	½ cup	¾ cup
Active sourdough starter	220 g	5 g	14 g	55 g	73 g	110 g	165 g
Sourdough discard	270 g	6 g	17 g	68 g	90 g	135 g	203 g

I also recommend getting in the habit of keeping 100 grams of your discard in the fridge for emergencies, swapping it out for newer discard once a week. You never know when you'll accidentally use up all your starter or spill the entire container on your kitchen floor. Some backup means you won't have to build again from scratch. Of course, the most wonderful thing you can do with your discard is to give it to a friend with feeding instructions, so they can get bit by the sourdough bug as well. Now that you've got a healthy starter going, you're ready to discover the sweet side of sourdough!

Levain Build

MAKES ENOUGH FOR
ONE 9-INCH (23-CM)
LOAF RECIPE, OR
210 GRAMS OF LEVAIN

70 ml (¼ cup plus 2 tsp)
room-temperature water

50 g (¼ cup) active sourdough
starter, 100% hydration

90 g (⅔ cup) bread flour

Building a levain, sometimes called a preferment, is common in many sourdough recipes, and it's incredibly useful. Building a levain allows you to maintain a small amount of starter and use a portion of it to inoculate a larger quantity of flour and water for a specific recipe.

Levain builds can vary widely in their hydration depending on the final dough. This not only makes for a very manageable amount of starter, but because it uses such a small quantity, the sour flavor is restrained and mellow—ideal for sweeter, enriched doughs. Since all sourdough starters are unique, the maturation time varies widely—anywhere from 6 to 12 hours—so keep an eye on it the first time.

And timing is everything. Generally, I like to feed my starter first thing so I can build my levain early in the day. This allows me to mix a dough in the evening and give it a few hours at room temperature before transferring it to the fridge overnight. The next morning, I can shape and bake. To figure out what timing will work best for you, get familiar with your starter's growth times and work backwards from when you'd ideally like to enjoy the final product. This formula appears in multiple enriched recipes in this book, and you can easily refer back to it.

In a small mixing bowl, combine the water and the active sourdough starter. Add the bread flour and bring the mixture together, kneading by hand if necessary, until uniform. Transfer the mixture to a clear jar or plastic container, 16-ounce (480-ml) capacity or larger.

Cover and set the container in a warm spot to double in volume, at least 6 hours and up to 12 hours. Use a rubber band or piece of tape to mark the starting volume and watch its progress. When it's doubled in volume, it's ready to use.

SWEET BREADS, BUNS and LOAVES

Bread is obviously the first thing that comes to mind when we talk about sourdough, and I've come to love incorporating my starter into sweeter doughs, pairing them with flavorful sugars, glazes, chocolates and fillings. These recipes are some of the most enticing in the book: Honey-Glazed Pull-Apart Bread (page 20), Cinnamon-Caramel Challah Knots (page 29), Chocolate–Peanut Butter Glazed Buns (page 38) and don't get me started on the Lemon-Poppy Cream Cheese Babka (page 26). To say these are the recipes of my dreams would be an understatement.

Honey-Glazed Pull-Apart Bread

MAKES ONE 9-INCH
(23-CM) LOAF

Dough

1 levain build, doubled in size
(page 17)

325 g (2½ cups plus 1½ tbsp)
all-purpose flour

114 g (1 stick) unsalted butter,
softened at room temperature

50 g (¼ cup) granulated sugar

2 large whole eggs

1 large egg yolk

24 ml (1 tbsp plus 2 tsp) whole
milk, at room temperature

1 tsp kosher salt

Let's talk about the pure tactile joy of a pull-apart bread: Layer upon layer of enriched dough, with warm, soft and fluffy insides. This sweet brioche-style loaf is a blast to eat, as you get to peel away the sweet, buttery sheets one by one. The honey glaze adds that perfect amount of sweetness that seeps between each sheet of dough. Its flavors are simple, warm and comforting, and you won't mind having a loaf of this around to snack on. For a mellow sourdough flavor, it relies on a levain build (see page 17). And with the not-insignificant amount of fat in the dough, it requires a long, slow fermentation and proofing. I recommend building the levain as early in the day as possible, then you can mix the dough in the afternoon or evening and shape and bake the following day. It's gonna be worth every soft, buttery, warm layer.

To make the dough: In the bowl of a stand mixer with the dough hook, combine the levain, flour, soft butter, sugar, whole eggs, egg yolk, milk and salt. Knead on low speed for 25 to 30 minutes, stopping the mixer and scraping it down every 10 minutes or so to make sure everything is getting incorporated, until the dough comes together in a smooth ball and pulls away from the sides of the bowl. The long kneading time is necessary for proper gluten development. It'll start off looking very shaggy and messy, but resist the urge to add additional flour before it magically smooths itself out!

Transfer the dough to a large bowl coated very lightly with neutral nonstick cooking spray. Cover and set in a warm spot, letting the dough proof for 4 hours at room temperature. It may not rise much this first proofing; that's OK! Gently fold the dough over itself, cover and transfer to the fridge to ferment overnight, 12 to 14 hours.

Spray a 9 x 4 x 4-inch (23 x 10 x 10-cm) loaf pan with neutral nonstick cooking spray and set aside. Remove the dough from the fridge and gently turn it out onto a floured work surface. Dust the top of the dough lightly with flour and gently roll it out into an 8 x 18-inch (20 x 46-cm) rectangle.

(continued)

Honey-Glazed Pull-Apart Bread (Continued)

Filling

57 g (4 tbsp) unsalted butter, softened at room temperature

39 g (3 tbsp) granulated sugar

Pinch of kosher salt

Glaze

30 ml (2 tbsp) honey

30 ml (2 tbsp) whole milk

24 g (3 tbsp) powdered sugar

Flaky sea salt, to garnish

To make the filling: Spread the soft butter all over the dough in a thin, even layer. Combine the sugar and salt in a small bowl; evenly dust the mixture over the butter. Using a pizza cutter or large knife, cut the rectangle into 24 small squares. I do this by cutting it 3 x 8, first dividing it into three 18-inch (46-cm)-long strips, and then slicing those each into eight even pieces. Stack the pieces of dough, a few at a time, and line them up in the bottom of the prepared pan, so they're all standing on edge. Once all the dough is stacked in the pan, cover it loosely with a piece of plastic. Place the loaf in a warm spot and proof until the rectangles have increased in size by about a third and appear light and puffy, 3 to 4 hours.

Heat the oven to 350°F (177°C) with a rack in the center. When fully proofed, uncover and transfer the loaf to the oven and bake until it's a deep golden brown on top, 45 to 55 minutes. Remove the loaf from the oven and allow to cool at room temperature in the pan.

To make the glaze: In a small saucepan, bring the honey and milk to a boil. Remove from the heat. Whisk in the powdered sugar until smooth.

After the loaf has cooled slightly but is still warm to the touch, gently remove it from the pan and place on a cutting board or platter. With a pastry brush, gently brush the top of the loaf with about half the honey glaze. Let it sit for 5 minutes, then add a second coat of glaze and garnish with the flaky sea salt. Pull apart and enjoy while still warm.

Dark Chocolate–Walnut Boule

MAKES 1 LARGE LOAF

368 ml (1½ cups plus 1 tbsp) water

93 g (⅓ cup plus 1½ tbsp) active sourdough starter

438 g (3 cups plus 3 tbsp) bread flour, divided

44 g (½ cup) Dutch process cocoa powder, sifted

45 ml (3 tbsp) honey

11 g (1 tbsp plus 1 tsp) kosher salt

141 g (1¼ cups) chopped walnut pieces

54 g (⅓ cup) finely chopped dark chocolate chunks, 60% to 70%

Rice flour, as needed

All-purpose flour, as needed

I love how this dramatic loaf walks the line between sweet and savory, even with dark chocolate being the star. The cocoa powder gives it an incredible earthy depth and complexity, and it's studded with buttery walnuts and chunks of dark chocolate, while honey rounds it all out. It's a real moody-looking showstopper with that classic, rustic sourdough crust. Enjoy it as is, or spread with everything from butter to soft cheeses, nut butters or honey. The next day, it toasts up like a dream.

In a large mixing bowl, combine the water with the sourdough starter and add half the bread flour (eyeballed is fine). With your hands, mix to combine. It will be a batter-like consistency. Cover and rest at room temperature for 30 minutes.

In another mixing bowl, combine the cocoa powder with the remaining bread flour. Mix until uniform. After 30 minutes add the honey to the wet mixture and mix by hand to incorporate. Then add the flour-and-cocoa mixture. Mix by hand in the bowl until you form a sticky, uniform dough using a kneading motion. Scrape any dough off your hands with a bowl scraper. Cover and rest for 45 minutes at room temperature.

After 45 minutes, uncover and sprinkle the salt on top of the dough. With your fingers, dimple the dough repeatedly to start to incorporate the salt. Then fold and stretch the dough over itself for 1 minute, rotating the bowl as you go, to combine the ingredients and create some strength in the dough. You can use your hands or a bowl scraper to assist. It'll feel sticky at this stage. Cover and rest another 45 minutes at room temperature. Repeat the fold and stretch action three more times at 45-minute intervals.

Rest for another 45 minutes. In a small bowl, mix the walnuts and chocolate. Uncover the dough and incorporate the walnut-and-chocolate mixture, adding it in four additions, and kneading the dough in the bowl with each addition to incorporate. Cover and rest at room temperature for 2 hours.

(continued)

Dark Chocolate–Walnut Boule

(Continued)

Dust a proofing basket well with rice flour. Using a little all-purpose flour for dusting as needed, turn the dough out onto your work surface and gently, by hand, stretch it into a 12 x 12-inch (30 x 30-cm) square. Fold the corners into the center to meet and form a smaller square. Repeat for another smaller square, pinching the corners together to create a ball. Flip the ball of dough seam side down. Use your hands and countertop to shape the dough into a smooth ball, creating some surface tension and a smooth, rounded top. Turning the dough over, gently placing it in the basket with the seam side up. Cover and transfer to the fridge to ferment for 14 to 18 hours. I like to do this overnight.

When you're ready to bake, place a Dutch oven with its lid on inside the oven with a rack in the center. Heat the oven to 500°F (260°C). When the oven comes to temperature, wait another 30 minutes to ensure the Dutch oven is as hot as possible.

Place a piece of parchment paper on your work surface and very gently invert the boule onto the paper, using your hand to help it land gently so it doesn't deflate. Using a bread lame or a sharp paring knife, score the loaf with one long swipe across the top of the loaf. If you like to get fancy with your scoring, go for it, but I usually keep mine on the simple side.

When ready, carefully remove the Dutch oven from the oven using potholders or towels. Place it on a heatproof surface and remove the hot lid. Using the parchment paper to lift, transfer the boule to the Dutch oven so the parchment lines the bottom. Replace the lid and return the pot to the oven.

Reduce the temperature to 480°F (249°C). Bake for 30 minutes, then remove the lid of the Dutch oven and reduce the heat to 465°F (241°C). Bake the loaf for another 20 minutes. The internal temperature should register 205 to 210°F (96 to 99°C) with a probe thermometer. Remove from the oven. Using large tongs or potholders, transfer the hot bread to a resting rack. Allow it to cool for at least 1 hour before slicing.

Lemon-Poppy Cream Cheese Babka

MAKES ONE 9-INCH
(23-CM) BABKA

Dough

1 levain build, doubled in size
(page 17)

325 g (2½ cups plus 1½ tbsp)
all-purpose flour

114 g (1 stick) unsalted butter,
softened at room temperature

50 g (¼ cup) granulated sugar

2 large whole eggs

1 large egg yolk

24 ml (1 tbsp plus 2 tsp) whole
milk, at room temperature

1 tsp kosher salt

Filling

226 g (8 oz) cream cheese

120 g (1 cup) powdered sugar

1 egg yolk

Zest of 2 lemons

Pinch of kosher salt

30 g (3 tbsp) poppy seeds

I've always gravitated toward the combination of lemon and poppy. It's such a perfect pairing and *always* visually appealing. When I was experimenting with different babka fillings, my friend Jessica (who styled and produced the photoshoot for this book!) suggested a Danish-like cream cheese filling, which I thought was pure genius. I made a test loaf ASAP and biked it over to her apartment to sample. I knew we had a winner when her three-year-old daughter, Michaela, devoured bite after bite. Thus, this Lemon-Poppy Cream Cheese Babka was born. It's a bright surprise and the cream cheese gives the layers of dough a rich, satisfying creaminess. As with the other enriched doughs in the book, this one takes time, so plan accordingly.

To make the dough: In the bowl of a mixer with the dough hook, combine the levain, flour, soft butter, granulated sugar, whole eggs, egg yolk, milk and salt. Knead on low speed for 25 to 30 minutes, stopping the mixer and scraping it down every 10 minutes or so to make sure everything is getting incorporated, until the dough comes together in a smooth ball and pulls away from the sides of the bowl. The long kneading time is necessary for proper gluten development. It'll start off looking very shaggy and messy, but resist the urge to add additional flour before it magically smooths itself out!

Transfer the dough to a large bowl coated very lightly with neutral nonstick cooking spray. Cover and set in a warm spot, letting the dough proof for 4 hours at room temperature. It may not rise much this first proofing; that's OK! Gently fold the dough over itself, cover and transfer to the fridge to ferment overnight, 12 to 14 hours.

To make the filling: Combine the cream cheese, powdered sugar, egg yolk, lemon zest and salt in a mixing bowl. Cream together until smooth. You can make this just before shaping the dough or up to 1 day ahead of time. If you make it in advance, keep it refrigerated and bring it up to room temperature 2 hours before rolling the babka.

(continued)

Lemon-Poppy Cream Cheese Babka (Continued)

Glaze

60 ml (¼ cup) water

50 g (¼ cup) granulated sugar

Zest of 1 lemon

When the dough has fermented for about 12 hours, spray a 9 x 4 x 4-inch (23 x 10 x 10-cm) loaf pan with neutral nonstick cooking spray. Remove the dough from the fridge and gently turn it out onto a floured work surface. Dust the top of the dough lightly with flour and gently roll it out into a 10 x 20-inch (25 x 51-cm) rectangle, with the short end of the dough facing you. Spread all the filling over the dough in an even layer. Then dust evenly with the poppy seeds.

Roll the dough up starting with the short edge to form a 10-inch (25-cm)-long spiral. Cut the roll down the middle the long way, creating two 10-inch (25-cm)-long strips. Place the middle of one half on top of the middle of the other half—forming an X—then twist the strips around one another. Place the twisted dough in the pan, tucking in the ends. Spray the top of the babka lightly with a nonstick spray and cover loosely with plastic.

Place the babka in a warm spot and proof again, until it increases in size by about a third and is light and puffy in appearance, 3 to 4 hours. Heat the oven to 350°F (177°C) with a rack in the center. When fully proofed, transfer the babka to the oven and bake until a deep golden brown on top, 45 to 55 minutes.

To make the glaze: While the babka bakes, bring the water, sugar and lemon zest to a boil in a small pot. Boil for 2 minutes to reduce slightly, stirring occasionally. Remove from the heat.

Remove the babka from the oven and immediately pour the glaze over the top, using it all. When cooled to room temperature, gently unmold, slice and enjoy.

Cinnamon-Caramel Challah Knots

MAKES 12 KNOTS

Challah Levain Build

36 ml (2 tbsp plus 1 tsp) water

28 g (2 tbsp) active sourdough starter, 100% hydration (page 11)

75 g (½ cup plus 1 tbsp) all-purpose flour

Dough

213 g (1¾ cups) all-purpose flour

2 large eggs

30 ml (2 tbsp) water, at room temperature

30 ml (2 tbsp) canola oil

15 ml (1 tbsp) honey

13 g (1 tbsp) granulated sugar

¾ tsp kosher salt

Cinnamon Caramel

200 g (1 cup) granulated sugar

120 ml (½ cup) water

180 ml (¾ cup) heavy cream

60 ml (¼ cup) whole milk

Challah was the first bread I ever taught myself to make. I was in the seventh grade, and it turned out absolutely awful. I attempted two round loaves to break the Yom Kippur fast one New Year. They were dense, overdone, dry and just really, really bad—but I couldn't have been more proud of myself! Fortunately for you, my challah skills have improved over the last few decades, and these caramel challah knots are nothing but a joy. This is a sticky dough, rich with oil and egg, that's well worth the wait for these gooey, caramel-soaked treats. Note that this levain build varies from the others in this book.

To build the levain: In a small mixing bowl, combine the water and the active sourdough starter. Add the flour and mix to combine. It will be stiff and require some kneading to incorporate all the flour. Transfer it to a clear 16-ounce (480-ml) container, cover and mark its starting level with a rubber band or piece of tape. Set it in a warm spot to double in volume, typically 8 to 12 hours.

When it's doubled in size, mix the dough: In the bowl of a mixer with the dough hook, combine the flour, eggs, water, oil, honey, sugar, salt and all the levain. Mix on low, kneading until a smooth ball forms, 25 to 30 minutes. The long kneading time is necessary for proper gluten development. It'll start off looking very shaggy and messy, but resist the urge to add additional flour before it magically smooths itself out into a slick dough.

Transfer the dough to a large bowl coated very lightly with neutral nonstick cooking spray. Cover and set in a warm spot, letting the dough proof for 4 hours at room temperature. It may not rise much this first proofing; that's OK! Gently fold the dough over itself, cover and transfer to the fridge to ferment overnight, 12 to 14 hours.

To make the cinnamon caramel: Combine the sugar with the water in a small, deep pot. It should be the texture of wet sand, with no sugar crystals remaining on the sides of the pot. In another pot, set the heat to medium-high and scald the cream and milk, removing it from the heat when you see the first few bubbles forming on the surface, about 5 minutes. Set aside. Over high heat, cook the sugar to a light, honey-colored caramel, about 10 minutes. If you're new to caramel, you can use a candy thermometer. Watch it closely as once the sugar is fully dissolved, it will turn from clear syrup to caramel quickly. Do not stir or disturb the sugar until you see it start to change color, as I find this can cause crystallization.

(continued)

Cinnamon-Caramel Challah Knots (Continued)

Cinnamon Caramel (cont.)

57 g (4 tbsp) unsalted butter

6 g (2 tsp) ground cinnamon

1 tsp kosher salt

Flaky sea salt, to garnish

Once you see the first signs of caramelization, carefully swirl the syrup around in the pan a few times so it colors evenly. Once it takes on a whiskey hue and reads 355 to 360°F (179 to 182°C) on a thermometer, reduce the heat to low, and carefully drizzle in the cream and milk mixture. The caramel will bubble up vigorously as you do this, so add it slowly and with caution!

Add the butter all at once, stirring the caramel gently until the mixture is uniform, allowing it to simmer for 3 minutes to thicken. Stir in the cinnamon and salt. Remove from the heat and allow the caramel to cool in the pot. Transfer to a small container, cover and refrigerate overnight.

The next morning, remove the dough and the caramel from the fridge. Turn the dough out onto a lightly floured work surface and divide it into 12 equal pieces (weighing roughly 45 grams each), rolling each into a coil 8 inches (20 cm) long.

Spray a 12-cavity muffin tin with neutral nonstick cooking spray. Add 30 milliliters (2 heaping tbsp) of caramel to each cavity. It can be room temperature or still cold; distribute any remaining caramel evenly. Knot each piece of dough by wrapping it around your first and middle fingers and then pulling the end through the center. Drop one knot of challah into each cavity of the muffin tin, then lightly spray the top of each knot with nonstick spray and cover loosely with plastic to proof at room temperature until doubled in size, and light and puffy, about 3 hours.

Heat the oven to 350°F (177°C) with a rack in the center. When the knots have doubled in size, uncover, transfer to the oven and bake until golden, 25 to 30 minutes. Remove from the oven and allow them to cool for 3 minutes in the muffin tin.

Once they've cooled slightly, place a sheet pan on top of the muffin tin and, using potholders or dry towels, quickly invert the knots and remove the muffin tin, letting all the caramel drizzle out and on top of the knots. Use a small spatula to coax any remaining caramel out of the cavities and onto the knots. Garnish each knot with a pinch of flaky sea salt. Allow them to cool for another 10 minutes, then enjoy.

Orange-Pistachio Caramel Sticky Buns

MAKES 9 BUNS

I love a sticky bun so much. No kidding. This recipe was one of the first I wrote and tested, because I knew an iconic sourdough sticky bun was a must for this book. Pistachios came into play because I wanted to switch it up a bit from the classic pecan situation. And while I'm sure I'm not the first person to make a pistachio sticky bun, I was thrilled with how these flavors and textures all came together. The sweet sticky caramel seeps into all the enriched sourdough layers, with a perfect salty, citrusy pistachio crunch on top and an orange-laced, buttery interior. I like to eat them by slowly unraveling the spiral, saving the extra saturated center morsel as a super sweet last bite.

Dough

1 levain build, doubled in size (page 17)

325 g (2½ cups plus 1½ tbsp) all-purpose flour

114 g (1 stick) unsalted butter, softened at room temperature

50 g (¼ cup) granulated sugar

2 large whole eggs

1 large egg yolk

24 ml (1 tbsp plus 2 tsp) whole milk, at room temperature

1 tsp kosher salt

Caramel

63 g (½ cup plus 1 tbsp) granulated sugar

45 ml (3 tbsp) water

90 ml (¼ cup plus 2 tbsp) heavy cream

45 ml (3 tbsp) whole milk

14 g (1 tbsp) unsalted butter

¾ tsp kosher salt

To make the dough: In the bowl of a mixer fitted with the dough hook, combine the levain, flour, soft butter, sugar, whole eggs, egg yolk, milk and salt. Knead on low speed for 25 to 30 minutes, stopping the mixer and scraping it down every 10 minutes or so to make sure everything is getting incorporated, until the dough comes together in a smooth ball and pulls away from the sides of the bowl. The long kneading time is necessary for proper gluten development. It'll start off looking very shaggy and messy, but resist the urge to add additional flour before it magically smooths itself out!

Transfer the dough to a large bowl coated very lightly with neutral nonstick cooking spray. Cover and set in a warm spot, letting the dough proof for 4 hours at room temperature. It may not rise much this first proofing; that's OK! Gently fold the dough over itself, cover and transfer to the fridge to ferment overnight, 12 to 14 hours.

To make the caramel: Combine the sugar with the water in a small, deep pot. It should be the texture of wet sand with no sugar crystals remaining on the sides of the pot. In another pot, set the heat to medium-high and scald the cream and milk, removing it from the heat when you see the first few bubbles forming on the surface, about 5 minutes. Set aside. Over high heat, cook the sugar to a light, honey-colored caramel, about 10 minutes. If you're new to caramel, you can use a candy thermometer. Watch it closely as once the sugar is fully dissolved, it will turn from clear syrup to caramel quickly. Do not stir or disturb the sugar until you see it start to change color, as I find this can cause crystallization.

(continued)

Orange-Pistachio Caramel Sticky Buns (Continued)

Filling

50 g (½ cup) roughly chopped roasted, salted pistachios (if using unsalted, add ½ tsp kosher salt)

67 g (⅓ cup) granulated sugar

Zest of 1 large orange

114 g (1 stick) unsalted butter, softened at room temperature

Flaky sea salt, to garnish

Once you see the first signs of caramelization, carefully swirl the syrup around in the pan a few times so it colors evenly. When it takes on a whiskey hue and reads 355 to 360°F (179 to 182°C) on a thermometer, reduce the heat to low and slowly and carefully drizzle in the cream-and-milk mixture.

Add the butter all at once, stirring the caramel gently until the mixture is uniform, allowing it to simmer for 3 minutes to thicken. Stir in the salt. Remove from the heat and allow the caramel to cool in the pot. Transfer to a small container, cover and refrigerate overnight, bringing to room temperature 1 hour before shaping the buns.

To make the filling: Line a 10-inch (25-cm) round cake pan with parchment paper and spray it with neutral nonstick cooking spray. Pour the caramel into the pan, tilting it so it covers the whole bottom. Add the chopped pistachios in an even layer. In a small bowl, combine the sugar and orange zest.

Remove the dough from the fridge and gently turn it out onto a floured work surface. Dust the top of the dough lightly with flour and gently roll the cold dough out into a 16 x 24-inch (41 x 61-cm) rectangle. Spread the soft butter on the dough in an even layer, then sprinkle with the sugar mixture. Roll the dough up into a spiral, starting with one long edge, and rolling it up to meet the other. With a sharp knife, cut the roll into nine pieces about 2½ inches (6 cm) thick. Place the spirals in the pan, swirls facing up.

Lightly spray the top of the rolls with the neutral nonstick cooking spray and cover loosely in plastic. Proof at room temperature until doubled in volume, puffy and light to the touch, 3 to 4 hours.

Heat the oven to 350°F (177°C) with a rack in the center. Uncover and transfer the fully proofed buns to the oven and bake until deep golden, 35 to 40 minutes. Remove the buns from the oven and allow them to cool in the pan for 10 minutes to let the caramel set slightly. Then, while still warm, place a platter on top of the buns and, using potholders or dry towels, quickly flip and invert the sticky buns onto the platter, tapping to release if needed. Peel away and discard the parchment paper. Garnish with a little flaky salt. Cool another 15 minutes, then pull apart and enjoy.

Earl Grey Brown Butter Buns

MAKES 8 LARGE BUNS

I've been stealthily incorporating Earl Grey tea into my pastries for quite a while now. It has a floral, citrusy flavor with a pronounced perfume of bergamot that I find oh-so-compelling, yet perfectly subtle. It's not unfamiliar, but many people can't quite put their finger on it, and I love that little bit of mystery it lends to a baked good. Paired with nutty brown butter and tangy cream cheese frosting, these buns are a complex sensory adventure. They're an unexpected brunch treat!

Brown Butter

142 g (10 tbsp or 5 oz) unsalted butter

6 g (1 tbsp) loose-leaf Earl Grey tea leaves, or the contents of 3 tea bags

Dough

1 levain build, doubled in size (page 17)

325 g (2½ cups plus 1½ tbsp) all-purpose flour

114 g (1 stick) unsalted butter, softened at room temperature

50 g (¼ cup) granulated sugar

24 ml (1 tbsp plus 2 tsp) whole milk, at room temperature

6 g (1 tbsp) loose-leaf Earl Grey tea leaves, or the contents of three tea bags

2 large whole eggs

1 large egg yolk

1 tsp kosher salt

To make the brown butter: I like to do this right before mixing the dough or up to a day ahead of time. In a deep pot, melt the butter over medium-high heat, allowing it to come to a boil. Carefully boil and cook to a deep honey color, whisking frequently, 4 to 5 minutes, and reducing it to about 120 milliliters (4 oz). Remove from the heat, add the tea and allow it to cool in the pot for 1 hour. Pour the brown butter through a fine strainer to remove the tea. Transfer the brown butter to a small container, cover and place in the fridge to solidify.

To make the dough: In the bowl of a mixer with the dough hook, combine the levain, flour, soft butter, sugar, milk, tea leaves, whole eggs, egg yolk and salt. Knead on low speed for 25 to 30 minutes, stopping the mixer to scrape it down every 10 minutes or so to make sure everything is getting incorporated, until the dough comes together in a smooth ball and pulls away from the sides of the bowl. The long kneading time is necessary for proper gluten development. It'll start off looking very shaggy and messy, but resist the urge to add additional flour before it magically smooths itself out!

Transfer the dough to a large bowl coated very lightly with neutral nonstick cooking spray. Cover and set in a warm spot, letting the dough proof for 4 hours at room temperature. It may not rise much this first proofing; that's OK! Gently fold the dough over itself, cover, and transfer to the fridge to ferment overnight, 12 to 14 hours. Remove the brown butter from the fridge to soften at room temperature overnight.

When the dough has fermented for about 12 hours spray an 8 x 10-inch (20 x 25-cm) baking pan or dish with neutral nonstick cooking spray; set aside.

(continued)

Earl Grey Brown Butter Buns (Continued)

Filling

50 g (¼ cup) granulated sugar

Zest of 2 lemons

½ tsp kosher salt

Frosting

150 g (1¼ cups) powdered sugar

114 g (1 stick) unsalted butter, softened at room temperature

113 g (4 oz) cream cheese, room temperature

½ tsp kosher salt

½ tsp vanilla extract

15 ml (1 tbsp) lemon juice

To make the filling: In a small bowl, combine the granulated sugar, lemon zest and salt, mixing to combine. Remove the dough from the fridge and gently turn it out onto a floured work surface. Dust the top of the dough lightly with flour and gently roll it out into a 16 x 16-inch (41 x 41-cm) square. Spread the soft brown butter over the dough, and then sprinkle evenly with the lemon sugar. Roll the dough up into a spiral. With a sharp knife, cut the roll into slices about 2 inches (5 cm) thick for eight rolls, and line the sliced buns up in the pan, spirals facing up.

Lightly spray the top of the rolls with the neutral nonstick cooking spray and cover loosely in plastic. Allow them to proof at room temperature until doubled in volume, puffy and light to the touch, 2 to 4 hours.

Heat the oven to 350°F (177°C) with a rack in the center. Transfer the fully proofed buns to the oven and bake until golden, 30 to 35 minutes. Remove the buns from the oven and allow them to cool to room temperature before frosting.

To make the frosting: Combine the powdered sugar, soft butter, cream cheese, salt, vanilla and lemon juice in a medium mixing bowl. With hand beaters, cream together until the mixture is smooth and uniform, about 2 minutes. When the buns are cool, spread the frosting all over the top. Pull apart and enjoy.

Chocolate-Peanut Butter Glazed Buns

If I had to pick one true love to be by my side forever, the combination of chocolate and peanut butter would be it. We could spend the rest of our lives together, and we'd be really, really happy. It's rich, nostalgic and indulgent, and I'm never not in the mood for it. These buns are everything I love: a pillowy, enriched dough, an indulgent chocolate filling and a sweet and salty peanut butter glaze. I can't really think of anything more I want in life than these buns. OK, well a bunch of things, but this recipe is still pretty awesome.

MAKES 9 BUNS

Dough

1 levain build, doubled in size (page 17)

325 g (2½ cups plus 1½ tbsp) all-purpose flour

114 g (1 stick) unsalted butter, softened at room temperature

50 g (¼ cup) granulated sugar

2 large whole eggs

1 large egg yolk

24 ml (1 tbsp plus 2 tsp) whole milk, at room temperature

1 tsp kosher salt

Filling

170 g (6 oz) dark chocolate, roughly chopped

114 g (1 stick) unsalted butter, softened at room temperature

180 ml (¾ cup) heavy cream

1 tsp vanilla extract

67 g (⅓ cup) granulated sugar

¼ tsp kosher salt

To make the dough: In the bowl of a mixer with the dough hook, combine the levain, flour, soft butter, sugar, whole eggs, egg yolk, milk and salt. Knead on low speed for 25 to 30 minutes, stopping the mixer and scraping it down every 10 minutes or so to make sure everything is getting incorporated, until the dough comes together in a smooth ball and pulls away from the sides of the bowl. The long kneading time is necessary for proper gluten development. It'll start off looking very shaggy and messy, but resist the urge to add additional flour before it magically smooths itself out!

Transfer the dough to a large bowl coated very lightly with neutral nonstick cooking spray. Cover and set in a warm spot, letting the dough proof for 4 hours at room temperature. It may not rise much this first proofing; that's OK! Gently fold the dough over itself, cover and transfer to the fridge to ferment overnight, 12 to 14 hours.

To make the filling: Place the chocolate and butter in a heatproof mixing bowl and set aside. In a small pot, bring the cream, vanilla, sugar and salt to a simmer, stirring occasionally to help dissolve the sugar. As soon as a few bubbles appear on the surface, about 5 minutes, pour the hot cream mixture over the chocolate and butter. Let it sit for 3 minutes and then whisk vigorously until it becomes smooth. Cover and leave the filling in a cool spot overnight, but do not refrigerate or else it won't be spreadable.

After the dough has fermented, spray two jumbo six-cavity muffin tins with a neutral nonstick cooking spray, keeping in mind that you only need nine cavities. Set aside.

(continued)

Chocolate-Peanut Butter Glazed Buns (Continued)

Glaze

120 g (1 cup) powdered sugar

117 ml (½ cup) whole milk

194 g (¾ cup) all-natural creamy peanut butter

Pinch of kosher salt

49 g (⅓ cup) roughly chopped roasted, salted peanuts

Remove the dough from the fridge and gently turn it out onto a floured work surface. Dust the top of the dough lightly with flour and gently roll it out into a 12 x 24-inch (30 x 61-cm) rectangle. Spread the filling over the dough. Roll the dough up into a spiral, starting with one of the long edges and rolling it up to meet the other for a 24-inch (61-cm)-long roll. With a sharp knife, cut the roll into nine slices, each about 2½ inches (6 cm) thick, wiping the knife clean on a damp rag between each cut. Transfer each spiral to a cavity in the prepared jumbo muffin tins.

Lightly spray the top of the rolls with the neutral nonstick cooking spray and cover loosely in plastic. Allow them to proof at room temperature until doubled in volume, puffy and light to the touch, 2 to 4 hours.

Heat the oven to 350°F (177°C) with a rack in the center. Transfer the fully proofed buns to the oven and bake until golden, 35 to 40 minutes. Allow them to cool completely in the tins.

To make the glaze: Place the powdered sugar in a mixing bowl. In a pot over low heat, combine the milk, peanut butter and pinch of salt. Cook to fully dissolve the peanut butter, whisking constantly, about 3 minutes. Once the mixture is smooth, pour it over the powdered sugar and whisk until uniform and no lumps remain.

When the buns are cool, unmold each one and place them on a baking sheet. They should pop out easily, but you can use a butter knife or small offset spatula to coax them if needed. Pick each one up from the bottom and dunk it in the glaze, allowing the excess to drip back into the bowl. Place them back on the sheet pan. After the first coat, spoon the remaining glaze over the buns, distributing it evenly and using it all up. Finish each bun with a sprinkling of the chopped peanuts and allow the glaze to set for 10 minutes. Enjoy right away.

Note: If you don't have a jumbo muffin tin, you can use a standard muffin tin, using 18 cavities and cutting the dough into slices 1¼ inches (3 cm) thick. Bake for about 25 to 40 minutes.

Sesame Honey Boule

MAKES ONE LARGE LOAF

300 ml (1¼ cups) water, at room temperature

93 g (⅓ cup plus 2 tbsp) active sourdough starter

394 g (3 cups) bread flour, divided

30 g (¼ cup) whole wheat flour

12 g (1½ tbsp) rye flour

30 ml (2 tbsp) honey

11 g (1 tbsp plus 1 tsp) kosher salt

90 g (½ cup plus 2 tbsp) mixed black and white sesame seeds, divided

Rice flour, as needed

All-purpose flour, for shaping

This is my favorite crusty bread to have around for everyday snacking. It has a beautiful crumb, satisfying chew and an intense crust. It gets a little sweetness from the honey and a nice nuttiness from the sesame seeds. I like to think of it as an all-purpose bread that takes me so gracefully from breakfast to dinner. I've used it for everything from a killer grilled cheese to an eggy breakfast sandwich on the savory side to schmearing it with jam and butter for something sweet. I can't live without this one.

In a large mixing bowl, combine the water and active sourdough starter. Mix with your hand to break up the starter in the water. Add half of the bread flour (eyeballed is fine), the whole wheat flour and rye flour, mixing by hand to form a uniform paste. Cover and allow to rest for 30 minutes.

After 30 minutes, add the honey and remaining bread flour. Knead the dough together in the bowl until all the dry flour is incorporated and it forms a sticky, shaggy ball. Cover and rest 45 minutes.

After the first 45 minutes, sprinkle the salt over the dough and incorporate it by poking the dough several times with your fingertips. Then fold and stretch the dough over itself for 1 minute. Cover and rest 45 minutes.

After the second 45 minutes, uncover and add 72 grams (½ cup) of sesame seeds in four additions: sprinkle them over, folding and stretching the dough as you go until they're evenly incorporated. Cover and rest another 45 minutes. Fold and stretch again for 1 minute. Repeat this a total of four times after the addition of the sesame seeds, resting 45 minutes between each. After the fourth round, cover and rest for 2 hours.

Dust a proofing basket well with rice flour. Turn the dough out onto a lightly floured work surface and stretch it gently into a 12 x 12-inch (30 x 30-cm) square. Fold the corners into the center to meet and form a smaller square. Repeat for another smaller square, continuing to pinch the corners together to create a ball. Flip the ball of dough upside down. Use your hands and countertop to shape the dough into a smooth ball, creating some surface tension and a smooth, rounded top. Turning the dough upside down, gently place it in the basket, cover and transfer to the fridge to ferment for 14 to 18 hours. I like to do this overnight.

(continued)

Sesame Honey Boule
(Continued)

1 large egg white

15 ml (1 tbsp) water

In the morning, place a Dutch oven with its lid on inside the oven with a rack in the center. Heat the oven to 500°F (260°C). When the oven comes to temperature, wait another 30 minutes to ensure the Dutch oven is as hot as possible.

Beat the egg white with the water in a small bowl and set aside. Place a piece of parchment paper on your work surface and very gently invert the boule onto the paper, using your hand to help it land gently so it doesn't deflate. Using a lame or a sharp paring knife, score the loaf with one long swipe across the top of the dough. If you like to get fancy with your scoring go for it, but I usually keep mine pretty simple. Gently brush the egg white mixture over the surface of the boule, then cover with the remaining 18 grams (2 tbsp) of sesame seeds.

When ready, carefully remove the Dutch oven from the oven using potholders or towels. Place it on a heatproof surface and remove the hot lid. Using the parchment paper to lift, transfer the boule to the Dutch oven, so the parchment lines the bottom. Replace the lid and transfer the pot to the oven. Reduce the heat to 475°F (245°C). Bake for 25 minutes, then remove the lid of the Dutch oven and reduce the heat to 465°F (240°C). Bake the loaf for another 25 minutes, or until the internal temperature reads 205 to 210°F (96 to 99°C). Remove the Dutch oven from the oven, and using large tongs or potholders, transfer the hot bread to a resting rack. Allow it to cool for at least 1 hour before slicing.

Peach and Ricotta Focaccia

This focaccia is the kind of thing I imagine I'd make while summering at a Tuscan villa, with soft, juicy peaches from a nearby orchard, creamy local ricotta and drizzles of golden-green olive oil and honey from the farmer down the road. But I've never even been to a Tuscan villa, so what do I know? I *do* know that this focaccia is a delicious balance of sour and sweet and will make you feel incredibly classy if you whip it up for an Aperitivo hour.

MAKES ONE 13 X 18-INCH (33 X 46-CM) FOCACCIA

480 ml (2 cups plus 1 tsp) water, at room temperature

150 g (scant ¾ cup) active sourdough starter

600 g (4¾ cups) all-purpose flour, divided

14 g (2 tbsp) kosher salt

60 ml (¼ cup) extra virgin olive oil, plus more for drizzling

In a large mixing bowl, combine the water and active starter, mixing well with your hands. Add half the flour (eyeballed is fine) and mix well; a few lumps are OK. It will be the consistency of pancake batter. Cover and let sit at room temperature for 30 minutes.

After 30 minutes, add the remaining flour and salt. Mix until uniform using your hands. The dough will be quite sticky at this stage; bring it together in the center of the bowl, using a bowl scraper to assist. Then cover and leave to rest for 1 hour at room temperature.

After the first hour, stretch and fold the dough for 1 minute in the bowl using a bowl scraper, turning the bowl as you go so it folds from a different direction each time. Cover and rest for 1 hour. Do this three more times. You'll need a total of four sets of folds.

After the last set of folds, cover the dough in the bowl and transfer to the fridge to ferment overnight, at least 10 hours and up to 14 hours.

In the morning, generously oil a 1-inch (2.5-cm)-deep, 13 x 18-inch (33 x 46-cm) aluminum sheet pan with 60 milliliters (¼ cup) of olive oil, spreading it evenly across the bottom and sides of the pan. Gently transfer the dough to the pan using a bowl scraper and fold it over itself once, then, using your fingers, gently press it out to a rectangle shape, coming to about 2 inches (5 cm) from the edges of the pan. The oil should pool nicely in the corners and little divots on top of the dough. Cover and place in a warm spot for 1 hour.

(continued)

Peach and Ricotta Focaccia
(Continued)

226 g (1 cup) fresh, whole milk ricotta

2 ripe yellow peaches, sliced ⅛ inch (3 mm) thick

15 ml (1 tbsp) honey

Flaky sea salt, to garnish

After 1 hour you should see some bubbles on top and the dough should have increased its volume by about half. Gently press the dough out further so it reaches the corners of the pan and, using your hands, dollop the ricotta over the top. Arrange the peach slices over the dough in a single layer. Use your fingers to dimple the surface of the dough, pressing the ricotta and peaches down a bit, and finish it with another light drizzle of olive oil. Cover with a piece of plastic wrap, and place in a warm spot and proof another 30 to 40 minutes, or until you see more bubbles forming on the surface. Heat the oven to 450°F (232°C) with a rack in the center.

After the second proofing, transfer the focaccia to the oven and bake until golden and bubbly, browning deeply in a few spots, 35 to 40 minutes depending on your oven.

When done, remove from the oven and using tongs or a spatula, carefully remove the focaccia from the pan and transfer to a resting rack to cool. After 10 minutes, drizzle with honey and garnish with a sprinkle of flaky sea salt. Slice as desired, enjoying warm or at room temperature.

Salted Honey Focaccia

This focaccia is so simple, chewy and mouthwatering, and you'll probably eat the entire loaf in two days. Maybe even less. It's a perfect canvas for cheeses, jams, fruit, butter or olive oil, which helps it go so fast. Fortunately, this dough comes together without too much effort, which means you can whip up another batch easily. What a sweet dream.

MAKES ONE 9 X 13-INCH (23 X 33-CM) FOCACCIA

Dough

480 ml (2 cups plus 1 tsp) water, at room temperature

150 g (scant ¾ cup) active sourdough starter

600 g (4¾ cups) all-purpose flour, divided

14 g (2 tbsp) kosher salt

60 ml (¼ cup) extra virgin olive oil, plus more for drizzling

To make the dough: In a large mixing bowl, combine the water and active starter, mixing well with your hands. Add half the flour (eyeballed is fine) and mix well; a few lumps are OK. It will be the consistency of pancake batter. Cover and let sit at room temperature for 30 minutes.

After 30 minutes, add the remaining flour and salt. Mix until uniform using your hands. The dough will be quite sticky at this stage; bring it together in the center of the bowl, using a bowl scraper. Then cover and leave to rest for 1 hour at room temperature.

After the first hour, stretch and fold the dough for 1 minute in the bowl using a bowl scraper or your hands, turning the bowl as you go so it folds from a different direction each time. Cover and rest 1 hour. Do this three more times. You'll need a total of four sets of folds.

After the last set of folds, cover the dough in the bowl and transfer to the fridge to ferment overnight, at least 10 hours and up to 14 hours.

In the morning, generously oil a 2-inch (5-cm)-deep, 9 x 13-inch (23 x 33-cm) metal pan with 60 milliliters (¼ cup) of olive oil, spreading it evenly across the bottom and sides of the pan. Gently transfer the dough to the pan using a bowl scraper and fold it over itself once, then, using your fingers, gently press it out to a rectangle shape, coming to about 2 inches (5 cm) from the edges of the pan. The oil should pool nicely in the corners and little divots on top of the dough. Cover and place in a warm spot for 1 hour.

(continued)

Salted Honey Focaccia
(Continued)

Syrup

15 ml (1 tbsp) water

30 ml (2 tbsp) honey

Flaky sea salt, as needed

After 1 hour you should see some bubbles on top and the dough should have increased its volume by about half. Gently press the dough out further so it reaches the corners of the pan and, using your hands, dimple the surface of the dough. Finish it with another light drizzle of olive oil. Cover, place in a warm spot and proof for 1 hour, or until you see more bubbles forming on the surface.

Heat the oven to 450ºF (232ºC) with a rack in the center. When hot, transfer to the oven. Bake until golden and bubbly, browning deeply in a few spots, 30 to 40 minutes depending on your oven.

While it bakes, make the syrup: Combine the water with the honey in a small saucepan and bring to a simmer over medium-high heat. Turn off the heat and leave in the pot in a warm spot.

When the focaccia is done, carefully remove it from the pan using tongs or a spatula and transfer to a resting rack to continue cooling. With a pastry brush, liberally paint the honey syrup all over the focaccia, giving it two coats. Sprinkle liberally with flaky salt. Cool another 20 minutes before slicing.

Toasted Hazelnut– Coffee Banana Bread

I don't like bananas—or banana bread for that matter—and I realize this is an unpopular opinion. According to Google, everyone loves banana bread, and so I wanted to include one in this book for both the banana bread lovers and those who think they hate it (me)! After lots of trial and error, I found that by pairing banana with other flavors I love (and a little sourdough, of course), I was really starting to warm up to it. Hazelnut, coconut and strong coffee give this banana loaf an indulgent complexity and richness, which is pretty irresistible . . . even to all those supposed haters out there.

MAKES ONE 9-INCH (23-CM) LOAF

Loaf

114 g (1 stick) unsalted butter, softened at room temperature

73 g (½ cup) dark brown sugar, packed

67 g (⅓ cup) granulated sugar

2 large eggs

110 g (½ cup) active sourdough starter

1 tsp vanilla extract

125 g (1 cup) all-purpose flour

120 g (1 cup) whole wheat flour

67 g (½ cup) chopped, roasted hazelnuts

100 g (1 cup) sweetened, shredded coconut flakes

3 g (2 tsp) instant espresso powder

1 tsp kosher salt

1 tsp baking soda

1 tsp baking powder

355 g (1¾ cups) mashed, ripe bananas

To make the loaf: Heat the oven to 350ºF (177ºC) with a rack in the center. Spray a 9 x 4 x 4–inch (23 x 10 x 10–cm) loaf pan with a neutral nonstick cooking spray, and line with a 9 x 6–inch (23 x 15–cm) strip of parchment paper, leaving a 2-inch (5-cm) overhang on the longer sides. Set aside.

In a large mixing bowl, use a wooden spoon or hand beaters to cream the butter with the brown sugar and granulated sugar until uniform, about 1 minute. Add the eggs, sourdough starter and vanilla. Mix until incorporated evenly.

In another mixing bowl, combine the all-purpose flour, whole wheat flour, hazelnuts, coconut, espresso powder, salt, baking soda and baking powder. Mix to evenly distribute everything. Then, using a spatula, fold the dry ingredients into the wet, folding together until fully combined and no dry bits remain. Last, fold in the mashed banana until evenly distributed. Transfer the batter to the prepared pan, smoothing it out into an even layer with the spatula and immediately transfer it to the oven.

Bake until golden brown on top, set in the center and a cake tester or toothpick comes out clean, 60 to 70 minutes. Remove the loaf from the oven and allow it to cool to room temperature in the pan.

Glaze

150 g (1¼ cups) powdered sugar

28 g (2 tbsp) unsalted butter, melted

30 ml (2 tbsp) strong coffee

Pinch of kosher salt

34 g (¼ cup) chopped, roasted hazelnuts

6 g (1 tbsp) sweetened, shredded coconut flakes

To make the glaze: Combine the powdered sugar, melted butter, coffee and salt in a mixing bowl. Mix with a spatula until smooth and no lumps of powdered sugar remain.

Carefully remove the cooled loaf from the pan and place it on a cutting board. Pour the glaze across the top of the loaf, going down the center and letting it drip into place. Top with the hazelnuts and coconut and allow it to set for 15 minutes. Slice and enjoy.

BISCUITS, SCONES and MORNING SWEETS

I'm not a morning person, but breakfast baking holds a special place in my heart—and if I'm honest, a pastry will help me get out of bed a little faster. At one point in my career, I oversaw the daily pastries for a local café. I'd have the ovens on by 5 a.m. each morning, somehow managing to fill the pastry case at the café by 7 a.m. with biscuits, scones, doughnuts, tea cakes and muffins. It was an excruciating challenge and a hustle, and I've never consumed so much coffee, but I loved knowing my baked goods were part of the neighborhood's morning routine. It's a powerful feeling, inserting yourself into strangers' lives like that. These days, most of my breakfast baking happens at home, on my own time, and I've found that sourdough can really flex in the morning. Scones, biscuits, muffins and just about everything in the pancake family can take a healthy dose of starter as it amplifies flavor and texture in the best way possible. If these recipes help you become a bit more of a morning person, I'll consider my job done.

Sourdough Doughnuts

MAKES 12
DOUGHNUTS PLUS
DOUGHNUT HOLES

Dough

Double recipe levain build, doubled in size (page 17)

650 g (5¼ cups) all-purpose flour, plus more for rolling

226 g (2 sticks) unsalted butter, softened at room temperature

100 g (½ cup) granulated sugar

4 large whole eggs

2 large egg yolks

50 ml (3 tbsp plus 1 tsp) whole milk

6 g (2 tsp) kosher salt

2 liters (64 fl oz) canola oil, for frying

I fell in love with making doughnuts a couple of years ago. I'd have to arrive at work by 5 a.m. to have them proofed and fried up in time for the morning rush, but they were worth that early alarm. I easily fell in love with deep frying the supple, enriched dough and the endless toppings, glazes, sugars and filling options. Deep frying at home can be a big project. I get that. But these are totally worth it for a weekend indulgence. I love classics such as cinnamon sugar or a tangy buttermilk glaze, which are included here, but go wild once you're confident. To attempt a filled doughnut, leave the centers intact and wait for them to fully cool before piping in jam, custard or pastry cream. Note this recipe uses a double portion of the standard levain build (page 17), so simply double the ingredients and follow the same procedure.

To make the dough: In the bowl of a mixer with the dough hook, combine the levain, flour, soft butter, sugar, whole eggs, egg yolks, milk and salt. Knead on low speed for 25 to 30 minutes, stopping the mixer and scraping it down every 10 minutes or so to make sure everything is getting incorporated, until the dough comes together in a smooth ball and pulls away from the sides of the bowl. The long kneading time is necessary for proper gluten development. It'll start off looking very shaggy and messy, but resist the urge to add additional flour before it magically smooths itself out!

Transfer the dough to a large bowl coated very lightly with neutral nonstick cooking spray. Cover and set in a warm spot for 4 hours at room temperature. It may not rise much this first proofing; that's OK! Once proofed, gently fold the dough over itself, cover and transfer to the fridge overnight, 12 to 14 hours.

Once the dough has fermented, set up two sheet pans. Cut 12 squares of 3 x 3-inch (8 x 8-cm) parchment paper, and spray each very well with neutral nonstick cooking spray. Line them up on the sheet pans, without overlapping.

Remove the dough from the fridge and gently turn it out onto a floured work surface. Dust the top of the dough lightly with flour and gently roll it out into a circle about ½ inch (1 cm) thick. This dough rolls best cold. Using a 2½-inch (6-cm) round cutter, punch out circles of dough, cutting about 12 doughnuts. Use a tiny ¾-inch (2-cm) round cutter to punch out the centers, saving these as doughnut holes for testing the oil and snacking. You can leave some without holes for filled doughnuts, if desired.

(continued)

Sourdough Doughnuts
(Continued)

Cinnamon Sugar

400 g (2 cups) granulated sugar

16 g (2 tbsp) ground cinnamon

Pinch of kosher salt

Vanilla Buttermilk Glaze

240 g (2 cups) powdered sugar

160 ml (⅔ cup) buttermilk

1 tsp vanilla extract

Pinch of kosher salt

Place the cut doughnuts on the squares of parchment, giving each its own square. Place the holes on the sheet pans in the empty spaces. With any scrap dough you can punch out additional little doughnut holes. Save the remaining scrap to test the oil or fry it up as is; I love having it to snack on. Spray the doughnuts with a little nonstick spray and cover loosely with plastic. Allow them to proof at room temperature for 3 to 4 hours, until puffy, doubled in size and light to the touch.

While the doughnuts proof, you can set up your toppings. To make the cinnamon sugar: In a mixing bowl, combine the granulated sugar, cinnamon and a pinch of salt. Mix well and set aside.
To make the glaze: In another mixing bowl, whisk together the powdered sugar, buttermilk, vanilla and salt until smooth. It should be the consistency of thin pancake batter. Set aside.

When the doughnuts are soft to the touch and doubled in size, heat the oil in a deep pot fitted with a candy thermometer to 325 to 350°F (165 to 177°C). While it heats up, set up a sheet pan with a resting rack right by the stove. Keep a slotted spoon handy. You can test the oil with the doughnut holes or scraps of dough, which should float and gently bubble when they hit the hot oil.

When the oil is ready, pick up the doughnuts on their parchment paper squares and carefully place two to three doughnuts at a time into the hot oil. The parchment will separate itself from the doughnut and you can fish it out with the spoon and discard as you go. This makes transferring the doughnuts to the oil quite easy. You can carefully drop the doughnut holes in by hand as you go, adding a few to the oil at a time. Allow the doughnuts to fry for 1 to 2 minutes on each side, using the slotted spoon to flip them over, until golden brown. Use the spoon to transfer them to the resting rack when done. The doughnut holes will fry for about 2 minutes total. Repeat until all the doughnuts are fried.

If using the cinnamon sugar, toss the doughnuts in it while still warm. If using the glaze, wait until they're cooled to room temperature before dunking the top of each doughnut and placing them back on the resting rack to set for 15 minutes before enjoying.

Caramelized Blueberry - Basil Blintzes

I had forgotten about blintzes for a while, but now they're back in my life in a big way, and I couldn't be happier about it. This recipe uses the discard to make a thin pancake with a little sourness that balances the sweet filling and boozy berries perfectly. But the best part of these is the sugar that caramelizes during the second frying, creating a crunchy crust that gives way to the supple pancake and creamy filling. I'll never forget about blintzes again.

MAKES 6 TO 8 FILLED BLINTZES

Compote

283 g (10 oz) frozen blueberries, no need to thaw

50 g (¼ cup) granulated sugar

120 ml (½ cup) dry red wine

Batter

240 ml (1 cup) whole milk

135 g (½ cup) discard sourdough starter

2 large eggs

14 g (1 tbsp) melted butter, cooled slightly, plus about 42 g (3 tbsp) for frying, as needed

½ tsp kosher salt

125 g (1 cup) all-purpose flour

Butter, for pan

67 g (⅓ cup) granulated sugar, for rolling

Filling

453 g (16 oz) farmer's cheese or ricotta

26 g (2 tbsp) granulated sugar

Zest of 1 lemon

½ tsp vanilla extract

1 large egg yolk

Pinch of kosher salt

To make the compote: In a small saucepan, combine the blueberries, sugar and wine. Bring to a boil, then reduce to low heat. Simmer the compote until thick and syrupy, stirring occasionally, about 30 minutes. Turn off the heat and set aside.

Meanwhile, make the batter: In a mixing bowl whisk together the milk, discard sourdough starter, eggs, melted butter and salt. Add the flour gradually and mix until smooth. Let sit for 15 minutes at room temperature.

To make the filling: Combine the cheese, sugar, lemon zest, vanilla, egg yolk and salt in a small bowl. Mix with a spatula until smooth.

Heat an 8-inch (20-cm) nonstick or well-seasoned cast-iron skillet over medium-high heat with about 7 grams (½ tbsp) of butter. Swirl the butter around to coat the skillet well, pouring out any excess. It should sizzle, but not smoke. Add 80 milliliters (⅓ cup) of batter to the skillet, tilting it to spread out. If it doesn't spread easily, add 15 to 30 milliliters (1 to 2 tbsp) more of milk to the whole batch of batter. When the surface starts to set and no longer appears wet, about 1 minute, carefully flip the pancake using a spatula, cooking for 1 minute. Transfer the cooked pancake to a plate while you repeat the process with the remaining batter, stacking the pancakes as you go.

When all the batter is cooked, assemble the blintzes: Spread 67 grams (⅓ cup) of sugar on a large plate for coating. Place about 60 grams (¼ cup) of filling in the center of a pancake, spreading it out into a line running the length of the pancake, leaving a 1-inch (2.5-cm) border. Fold one edge into the center to cover the filling, fold in the sides 2 inches (5 cm) and then roll the whole thing up. Roll the blintz in the granulated sugar to coat lightly on all sides, then transfer to a plate while you repeat with the remaining pancakes and filling.

(continued)

Caramelized Blueberry - Basil Blintzes (Continued)

Topping

20 g (¼ cup) fresh, torn basil leaves

Zest of 1 lemon

Heat the skillet again with a little butter as before, over medium-high heat, then add the blintzes, two or three at a time, with the seam side down. Fry until golden, pressing down slightly with a spatula so they sear and caramelize on the first side, 2 to 4 minutes. Flip and cook the other side to caramelize, then transfer to a serving platter, reducing the heat to medium if they seem to brown too quickly.

Repeat with the remaining blintzes, adding a little butter as needed if the pan gets dry. If caramelized sugar starts to build up in the pan, wipe it out with a paper towel and add more butter before proceeding. If the pan smokes, remove the pan from the burner for a moment and turn the heat down to low.

When done caramelizing, spoon the compote over the blintzes. Garnish with fresh basil and lemon zest and serve right away.

Sweet Cream Biscuits

MAKES 6 BISCUITS

188 g (1½ cups) all-purpose flour, plus a little for your work surface

14 g (1 tbsp) baking powder

¾ tsp kosher salt

50 g (4 tbsp) sugar, divided

114 g (1 stick) chilled unsalted butter, cut into ½-inch (1-cm) cubes

220 g (1 cup) active sourdough starter

132 ml (½ cup plus 1 tbsp) heavy cream, divided

½ tsp ground cinnamon (optional)

I love a sweet biscuit, and for as long as I can remember, I've made mine with heavy cream. Its sweet richness balances out the tangy sourdough and makes for a super fatty—meaning delicious—and balanced biscuit. A brunch staple, my favorite way to enjoy these is slathered with butter and jam, but they can stand up to a savory breakfast sandwich just as well. And I'll never complain about one on its own either. The cinnamon sugar on top is optional, but highly recommended.

In a mixing bowl, combine the flour, baking powder, salt and 37 grams (3 tbsp) of sugar. Mix well to combine and then add the butter. With your hands or pastry cutter, work the butter into the flour until all the pieces are pea-sized and the mixture looks crumbly.

In a small bowl, beat the sourdough starter and 120 milliliters (½ cup) of cream together with a fork just to combine. Add it to the dry mixture and fold by hand until it just holds together. It'll look messy and shaggy.

Turn the dough out onto a lightly floured work surface. With your hands, shape the dough into a rectangle and gently roll it out to about ½ inch (1 cm) thick. Fold the dough in half, bringing the shorter ends together, rotate it 90 degrees and repeat, rolling it out and folding it in half again. Do this rolling, folding and rotating until you've done five folds and six full turns of the dough, dusting with a little all-purpose flour as needed if the dough is getting sticky.

After the last turn, line a sheet pan with parchment paper. Roll the dough out to a 1½-inch (4-cm)-thick rectangle, about 8 x 6 inches (20 x 15 cm), and with a sharp knife, cut into squares for six biscuits. Transfer the biscuits to the prepared pan and place in the freezer to chill for 30 minutes to 1 hour.

Heat the oven 375°F (190°C) with a rack in the center. Take the biscuits out of the freezer. Brush the top of each biscuit with the remaining 12 milliliters (1 tbsp) of heavy cream using a pastry brush or your fingers. Mix the remaining 13 grams (1 tbsp) of sugar with the cinnamon, if using, and sprinkle the mixture on top of each biscuit. Transfer to the oven and bake until golden, 35 to 40 minutes. Allow the biscuits to cool on the pan for 10 minutes. Enjoy warm.

Jammy Ricotta Drops

MAKES 8 TO 10 DROPS

219 g (1¾ cups) all-purpose flour

50 g (4 tbsp) granulated sugar, divided

14 g (1 tbsp) baking powder

¾ tsp kosher salt

114 g (1 stick) chilled unsalted butter, cut into ½-inch (1-cm) cubes

340 g (12 oz or about 1⅓ cups) fresh, whole-milk ricotta cheese

78 g (⅓ cup) active sourdough starter, 100% hydration (page 11)

60 ml (¼ cup) chilled buttermilk

240 g (¾ cup) jam, any variety or a mix of a few

Not quite a biscuit, not really a pastry, these rustic, jammy drops were inspired by thoughts of thumbprint cookies, drop biscuits and fruit Danishes all swirling in my head. I loved the idea of baking the jam right into the dough. And the ricotta is rich and delicious against the tart sourdough and buttermilk. I like to mix these up with whatever jams I have around, making a few of each flavor and leaving some plain to enjoy with butter. Apricot and sour cherry are my favorite, but I know you'll do what you love with them.

Heat the oven to 350°F (177°C) with a rack in the center. Line two half sheet trays with parchment paper and set aside. In a mixing bowl combine the flour, 37 grams (3 tbsp) of sugar, baking powder and salt. Whisk to combine. With your hands or pastry cutter, work the butter into the flour until all the pieces are pea-sized and the mixture looks crumbly. Add the ricotta, starter and buttermilk at once and gently fold the mixture until it just holds together. It will look messy, wet and a bit lumpy.

Using a ⅓-cup (80-ml) measure, drop dollops of dough onto the sheet pans, spacing them about 2½ inches (6 cm) apart as they will spread considerably. Use a small spatula or your finger to help coax the dough out of the measuring cup. Using the back of a spoon or your fingers, create a little well in each, or leave any alone you want to enjoy plain. Fill each well with 15 milliliters (1 tbsp) of jam. Sprinkle the remaining 13 grams (1 tbsp) of granulated sugar over the tops of the drops and transfer to the oven. Bake until golden, 35 to 40 minutes. Allow them to cool for at least 10 minutes before serving.

Lemon-Almond Crème Fraîche Scones

MAKES 6 LARGE SCONES

I came up with the non-sourdough version of this scone years ago when I wanted something that was just sweet enough for a weekday breakfast, but not over the top. Lemon always makes my mouth water and balances sugar so well that I'll always go back for more. Turns out that adding sourdough starter was such a welcomed update. The crème fraîche means they stay soft and moist, even the next day, so anyone who thinks they don't like scones because they tend to be dry will have no argument against these.

Dough

247 g (1¾ cups) all-purpose flour

60 g (½ cup) sliced almonds

50 g (¼ cup) granulated sugar

7 g (2 tsp) baking powder

½ tsp kosher salt

Zest of 2 lemons

114 g (1 stick) chilled unsalted butter, cut into ½-inch (1-cm) cubes

73 g (⅓ cup) active sourdough starter

73 ml (⅓ cup) heavy cream, chilled

86 g (⅓ cup) crème fraîche, chilled

To make the dough: Line a sheet pan with parchment paper and set aside. In a mixing bowl combine the flour, almonds, sugar, baking powder, salt and lemon zest. Mix to combine and evenly distribute everything.

Add the cold butter and with your hands or pastry cutter, work it into the flour until all the pieces are pea-sized and the mixture looks crumbly. In a small bowl, combine the sourdough starter, heavy cream and crème fraîche with a fork. Add it to the dry butter mixture and fold them together with a spatula until no dry patches remain. It will look shaggy.

Heat the oven to 350°F (177°C) with a rack in the center. Turn the dough out onto a floured work surface and shape the dough into a disc, 6½ inches (17 cm) in diameter and about 1½ inches (4 cm) thick. Wrap the disc in plastic and refrigerate for 20 minutes. Then unwrap and with a knife slice it into six triangles, like you're slicing a cake. Transfer the triangles to the prepared sheet pan, spacing them out evenly in two rows. Bake until golden brown all over, 40 to 45 minutes.

(continued)

Glaze

150 g (1¼ cups) powdered sugar

30 ml (2 tbsp) lemon juice, or more as needed (from 1 to 2 lemons)

Pinch of kosher salt

30 g (¼ cup) sliced almonds, lightly toasted, to garnish

While the scones bake, make the glaze: In a mixing bowl combine the powdered sugar, lemon juice and salt. Mix with a spatula until smooth, adding a little extra lemon juice if you prefer a thinner glaze.

When done, remove the scones from the oven and allow them to cool to room temperature. When cooled, spoon or drizzle the glaze over the tops and finish with a few toasted almond slices.

Lemon Sugar Crêpes

MAKES 6 TO 8 CRÊPES

270 g (1 cup) discard sourdough starter

60 ml (¼ cup) whole milk

2 large eggs

16 g (2 tbsp) all-purpose flour

28 g (2 tbsp) melted butter, plus additional solid butter for frying, as needed

13 g plus 50 g (1 tbsp plus ¼ cup) granulated sugar, divided

½ tsp kosher salt

Zest of 2 lemons

Butter, for pan

One of my most vivid food memories is my first crêpe, with lemon and sugar, in Paris when I was eleven years old, that my mom forced me to order in my sixth-grade-level French. I stood there and was mesmerized by the batter hitting the hot griddle, spreading out into a paper-thin layer that cooked in seconds. The granulated sugar partially dissolved in the fresh-squeezed lemon juice against the warmth of the translucent pancake, but still retained a little bit of crunch. The sweet with the sour popped in my mouth and I was floored that something so simple could be so mouthwatering. To this day I love simple sweets like this and their ability to surprise and comfort us simultaneously. While sourdough isn't traditional in French-style crêpes, I find you can use the discard in them and it works so well, which gives you an excuse to eat more crêpes—bonus! I love eating these with a little crème fraîche on the side; you should do the same.

In a mixing bowl, whisk together the discard sourdough starter, milk, eggs, flour, melted butter, 13 grams (1 tbsp) of sugar and salt. Cover and transfer the mixture to the fridge for 1 hour. In a small mixing bowl, combine the 50 grams (¼ cup) of sugar with the lemon zest and set aside.

When you're ready to cook the crêpes, set up a sheet pan with a fitted resting rack next to the stove. On the stove over medium-high heat, melt about 7 grams (1½ tsp) of butter in an 8- to 10-inch (20- to 25-cm) nonstick skillet. When the butter is fully melted and coats the bottom of the pan, tip out any extra butter so just a thin film remains and wipe quickly with a paper towel. Add about 80 milliliters (⅓ cup) of the batter, rotating the pan to swirl it out into a thin, even layer. Cook the crêpe for about 2 minutes, until golden on the bottom, then flip using a spatula or tongs.

(continued)

Lemon Sugar Crêpes
(Continued)

Powdered sugar, for dusting

Lemon wedges, for serving

Crème fraîche, to garnish (optional)

While the other side cooks, sprinkle the cooked side with an even, thin layer of the lemon sugar, about 8 grams (2 tsp) per crêpe. Cook for about 1 minute; check the bottom using a spatula or tongs—it should be just turning golden. Fold the crêpe in half and then into a quarter using a spatula. Transfer it to the sheet pan using a spatula or tongs while you repeat the process with the remaining batter. Add small amounts of butter to the skillet as needed so the crêpes don't stick, transferring finished ones to the sheet pan as they finish cooking. If the skillet smokes or gets too hot, turn the heat down.

Once all the crêpes are cooked, they can be plated and enjoyed at room temperature, dusted with powdered sugar and served with lemon wedges, or dolloped with crème fraîche if desired. Alternatively, they can be reheated on the sheet pan in a 300°F (150°C) oven for 10 minutes before serving.

Salted Dark Chocolate Chunk Scones

These dark chocolate sourdough scones are exceedingly delicious. You have to make them—I don't really know what else to say! They're super rich with butterfat from the cream and have savory undertones thanks to the sourdough starter—it's like getting to eat a giant cookie for breakfast. It's important to use a good-quality dark chocolate in the 60% to 70% range, and chunks are key— *never* chips—for the proper distribution. I love these scones so much. Just go make them!

MAKES 8 SCONES

180 g (1½ cups) all-purpose flour, plus a little for your work surface

114 g (1 stick) unsalted butter, cut into ½-inch (1-cm) cubes and chilled

39 g (3 tbsp) granulated sugar

14 g (1 tbsp) baking powder

¾ tsp kosher salt

170 g (1 cup) chopped dark chocolate, 60% to 70%

220 g (1 cup) active sourdough starter, 100% hydration (page 11)

104 ml (⅓ cup plus 2 tbsp) heavy cream

1 large egg, beaten

15 ml (1 tbsp) whole milk or water

Flaky sea salt, to garnish

In a mixing bowl, combine the flour, butter, sugar, baking powder and salt. With your hands or pastry cutter, work the butter into the flour until all the pieces are pea-sized and the mixture looks crumbly. Add the chopped chocolate chunks and mix to distribute it evenly.

In a small bowl, beat the sourdough starter and cream together with a fork just to combine. Add it to the dry mixture and fold by hand until it just holds together. It'll look messy and shaggy. Turn the dough out onto a lightly floured work surface. With your hands, shape the dough into a rectangle and with a rolling pin gently roll out to about ¾ inch (2 cm) thick. Fold the dough in half, bringing the shorter ends together, rotate it 90 degrees and repeat, rolling it out and folding it in half again. Do this rolling, folding and rotating pattern until you've done five full turns, dusting with flour as needed if the dough is getting sticky.

After the fifth fold, line a sheet pan with parchment paper. Roll out the dough to a 1½-inch (4-cm)-thick rectangle, measuring about 4½ x 9 inches (11 x 23 cm). Cut the rectangle into eight squares measuring 2½ inches (6 cm) each. Transfer the squares to the prepared pan, spaced 3 inches (8 cm) apart, and place in the freezer for 30 minutes or cover with plastic and freeze for up to 1 week.

Heat the oven 375°F (190°C) with a rack in the center. Take the scones out of the freezer. Beat the egg with the whole milk in a small bowl. Brush the top of each scone liberally using a pastry brush or your fingers. Sprinkle the tops with a pinch of flaky sea salt. Transfer to the oven and bake until golden, 35 to 40 minutes, with an additional 5 minutes if baking from frozen. Allow the scones to cool for at least 10 minutes before enjoying.

Sweet and Sour Cherry Dutch Baby

I've always felt like cherries are special. They have a short season, can be a little tricky to find and are always expensive. But above all, they're delicious and totally worth it. Combining fresh sweet ones with their sour, syrupy counterparts on top of this giant, dramatic sunken pancake makes me swoon. Incorporating air into the batter by blending and then letting it rest is key to get the proper rise and fall of a classic Dutch baby.

MAKES ONE 9-INCH (23-CM) PANCAKE

110 g (½ cup) active sourdough starter, 100% hydration (page 11)

60 ml (¼ cup) whole milk

57 g (4 tbsp) unsalted butter, melted

31 g (¼ cup) all-purpose flour

3 large eggs

26 g (2 tbsp) granulated sugar

1 tsp vanilla extract

¼ tsp kosher salt

14 g (1 tbsp) unsalted butter, room temperature

77 g (½ cup) jarred, pitted sour cherries, in light syrup, drained and cut in half

300 g (2 cups) fresh or thawed frozen sweet cherries, pitted and cut in half

Powdered sugar, for serving

Heat the oven to 425°F (220°C) with a rack in the center. Place a 9-inch (23-cm) cast-iron skillet in the oven to heat up while you mix the batter.

In a large bowl, combine the sourdough starter, milk, melted butter, flour, eggs, sugar, vanilla and salt. Using an immersion blender or transferring to a standing blender, blend the batter until uniform and frothy, about 3 minutes. Let the batter sit for 15 minutes, then blend it again for 1 minute.

Carefully remove the hot skillet from the oven and place it on a heatproof surface. Add the room temperature butter and swirl it around so it melts and coats the pan. Add the batter to the hot skillet and return the pan to the oven. Bake until puffy and golden brown around the edges, 20 to 25 minutes.

Remove the Dutch baby from the oven and top with the cherries as the pancake naturally falls. Finish with a liberal dusting of powdered sugar, using a small, fine strainer. Slice and enjoy right away directly from the pan.

Fluffy Sunday Pancakes

MAKES APPROXIMATELY A DOZEN PANCAKES

2 large eggs, separated

156 g (1¼ cups) all-purpose flour

30 g (¼ cup) whole wheat flour

26 g (2 tbsp) granulated sugar

1 tsp kosher salt

1 tsp baking powder

300 ml (1¼ cups) whole milk

220 g (1 cup) active sourdough starter

28 g (2 tbsp) melted butter

Butter or neutral oil, for the skillet or griddle

Additions such as berries, whipped cream, nuts, chocolate chips, etc. (optional)

Sourdough pancakes have been done 8,273,912 times. No one really cares about them anymore. But I do. *I* care. And these are different—they're the main event, not an afterthought using the discard—no disrespect! Using active starter along with whipping the egg whites separately works some real magic here, and yeah, it's a little fussy, I'll admit, but they're worth the effort. For the ultimate fluff factor, don't let the batter sit. You'll want to get them in the pan right away. Once you have them on the heat and they start to set, dot them with berries, chocolate chunks, chopped fruit or nuts, or keep them plain and simple. Maple syrup, butter and whipped cream are all welcome. Note this recipe can be easily doubled, because sometimes you just need a lot of pancakes.

Place the egg whites in a mixing bowl and with a whisk or handheld beaters, whip them to stiff peaks. In a separate mixing bowl, combine both flours with the sugar, salt and baking powder. Add the egg yolks, milk and sourdough starter and gently fold together with a spatula until uniform. Fold in the melted butter.

With the spatula, add the whipped whites in three additions, gently folding them in until uniform; a few little streaks here and there is fine.

Heat the oven to 300°F (149°C) with a rack in the center. Line a sheet pan with parchment paper. Heat a 10-inch (25-cm) cast-iron or nonstick skillet or a griddle over medium-high heat. Add just enough butter or oil to coat the surface. Use a ⅓-cup (80-ml) measure to scoop the batter into pools on the hot pan or griddle. Once the edges start to set and you see little bubbles forming across the surface, about 1 minute, add any additions, if using, and then gently flip using a spatula. Cook for 1 to 2 minutes, or until golden on the bottom, then transfer the finished pancakes to the sheet pan.

Place the sheet pan in the oven to keep the pancakes warm as you cook the rest, adding them to the oven as you go. Serve warm with syrup, soft butter, berries, whipped cream and anything else you fancy.

Pumpkin Muffins

MAKES 12 MUFFINS

I've come full circle with my relationship to pumpkin baked goods. I loved them, then overdid it in every sense and avoided them for years, and now am falling in love again—especially with the addition of sourdough. The best part of this pumpkin treat is the incredibly crunchy streusel topping that gives way to a soft, lightly spiced coffee cake with a delicate sourdough crumb. They're great fresh out of the oven and equally delicious griddled with butter a day or two later.

Streusel

63 g (½ cup) all-purpose flour

67 g (⅓ cup) granulated sugar

35 g (¼ cup) pumpkin seeds

¼ tsp kosher salt

¼ tsp ground cinnamon

28 g (2 tbsp) unsalted butter, melted

34 g (2 tbsp) discard sourdough starter

Muffin

200 g (1 cup) granulated sugar

90 ml (⅓ cup plus 4 tsp) canola or grapeseed oil

2 large eggs

¾ tsp vanilla extract

184 g (¾ cup) pumpkin puree

110 g (½ cup) active sourdough starter

141 g (1 cup plus 2 tbsp) all-purpose flour

9 g (1½ tsp) kosher salt

7 g (1½ tsp) baking powder

¾ tsp baking soda

¾ tsp ground cinnamon

¾ tsp ground ginger

¼ tsp ground cardamom

Powdered sugar, to garnish

To make the streusel topping: In a mixing bowl, combine the flour, sugar, pumpkin seeds, salt and cinnamon. Mix to combine. Add the melted butter and discard sourdough starter. Mix with a spatula until no dry bits remain and the mixture is crumbly, with marble to pea-sized bits. Transfer to the fridge to chill while you mix the batter.

To make the muffins: Heat the oven to 350°F (177°C) with a rack in the center. Spray a 12-cavity muffin tin with neutral nonstick cooking spray or use liners and set aside. In a mixing bowl with a whisk, mix the sugar and oil until fully combined. Add the eggs and vanilla. Mix well. Add the pumpkin and sourdough starter. Mix until uniform.

In a separate bowl, whisk together the flour, salt, baking powder, baking soda, cinnamon, ginger and cardamom. Using a spatula, gently fold the dry ingredients into the wet until fully incorporated.

Pour the batter equally into all 12 muffin cavities. Top each muffin with a generous handful of the streusel, pressing it into the batter and distributing it evenly over all the muffins. Bake until set, golden and fluffy and a cake tester or toothpick inserted into the center comes out clean, 25 to 30 minutes.

Allow the muffins to cool until they're easy to handle. Gently remove them from their pan, and dust liberally with powdered sugar using a small, fine strainer. Enjoy warm or at room temperature.

Jane's Morning Glory Muffins

MAKES 12 MUFFINS

61 g (½ cup) roughly chopped, dried cherries

180 ml (¾ cup) hot water

125 g (1 cup) all-purpose flour

90 g (¾ cup) whole wheat flour

165 g (¾ cup) dark brown sugar, packed

81 g (⅓ cup plus ¼ cup) pumpkin seeds, divided

47 g (½ cup) shredded, sweetened coconut flakes

59 g (½ cup) chopped walnuts

9 g (2 tsp) baking powder

12 g (2 tsp) kosher salt

1 tsp ground cinnamon

1 tsp ground ginger

160 ml (⅔ cup) olive oil

110 g (½ cup) active sourdough starter

3 large eggs

10 ml (2 tsp) vanilla extract

145 g (¾ cup) unpeeled and grated tart apple, such as Granny Smith

This recipe is dedicated to my sweet friend Jane who heart-breakingly left us far too soon. I had the privilege of knowing her personally and professionally, and she was a gifted baker who truly loved her work. She was a creative force in the kitchen with great energy and created this morning glory muffin recipe for our pastry program when we worked together. It quickly became a personal favorite, as well as a favorite for many customers. I loved how full of nuts and fruit it was, and I got into the habit of swiping one for myself several times a week, still warm, before the batch hit the pastry case. I've held onto the recipe for a while now and think of her every time I make a batch. This version with sourdough has the same good stuff Jane loved about her muffins, with a little something extra. This one's for you, sweet Jane! I think about you all the time.

Heat the oven to 350°F (177°C) with a rack in the center. Place the chopped cherries in a small bowl and pour the hot water over them. Set aside. Spray a 12-cavity muffin tin with neutral nonstick cooking spray or use liners. Set aside.

In a mixing bowl, combine both the flours, brown sugar, 46 grams (⅓ cup) of pumpkin seeds, the coconut, walnuts, baking powder, salt, cinnamon and ginger. By hand or with a spatula, mix well and break up any clumps of brown sugar.

In a separate bowl, whisk the olive oil, sourdough starter, eggs and vanilla until uniform. Add the grated apple and mix through. Pour the wet mixture into the dry and gently fold together using a spatula, until the mixture is uniform and no dry patches remain.

Scoop the batter into the prepared pan, filling the cavities with about a heaping 60 milliliters (¼ cup) of batter each, distributing any remaining batter evenly. Top each with the remaining 35 grams (¼ cup) of pumpkin seeds. Bake until puffy and set, and a toothpick or cake tester comes out clean, 30 to 35 minutes.

Remove from the oven and allow the muffins to cool until easy to handle. Enjoy warm or room temperature.

PIES, TARTS, COBBLERS and CRUMBLES

I stand by the fact that pie and its close friends are some of the simplest, most foolproof baked goods one can attempt. Even a less than perfectly shaped crust has a rustic charm, and for novice home bakers, I often say a simple fruit galette is a great place to build some baking confidence. Sourdough makes an exceptionally crisp pie crust with a toothsome texture you'll find addictive—and you'll never get a soggy bottom! It is equally helpful in cobbler and crumble toppings, mingling with warm jammy fillings and cool dairy accompaniments. This chapter has everything from those simple, flaky galettes to pies, indulgent chocolate tarts, juicy cobblers and seasonal crumbles that will knock your socks off.

Blueberry–Lemon Thyme Cobbler

MAKES ONE 10-INCH (25-CM) COBBLER

Jammy blueberries shine in this simple cobbler. It's an accessible stepping-stone between a crumble and a pie that can be thrown together on a whim. I love the substantial sourdough biscuit topping that gives way to warm, luscious fruit—it gets me every time. I only make this when blueberries are in season, which makes it particularly special and delicious, and lemon thyme gives it a light, herbaceous lift. If you can't get your hands on lemon thyme, the standard variety will work, just use half the amount. I like to serve this with soft, unsweetened whipped cream, but ice cream is always a good move, too.

Filling

888 g (5 cups) fresh blueberries, rinsed and picked through for stems

150 g (¾ cup) granulated sugar

16 g (2 tbsp) cornstarch

Zest and juice of 1 lemon

1 tsp fresh lemon thyme leaves

Topping

125 g (1 cup) all-purpose flour

57 g (4 tbsp) chilled unsalted butter, cut into ½-inch (1-cm) cubes

26 g (2 tbsp) granulated sugar

2 tsp freshly picked lemon thyme leaves, plus a few for garnish if desired

1 tsp kosher salt

1 tsp baking powder

110 g (½ cup) active sourdough starter

240 ml (1 cup) heavy cream, divided

8 g (1 tbsp) powdered sugar (optional)

Heat the oven to 375°F (165°C) with a rack in the center. To make the filling: In a large mixing bowl, combine the berries, sugar, cornstarch, lemon zest, lemon juice and the lemon thyme. Mix to combine and set aside.

To make the topping: In a separate mixing bowl, combine the flour, cold butter cubes, granulated sugar, lemon thyme, salt and baking powder. With your hands, pinch the butter into the flour, until the mixture is crumbly and mealy. In a separate bowl, with a fork, whisk together the sourdough starter and 60 milliliters (¼ cup) of heavy cream. Add it to the dry mixture, folding everything together with a spatula until incorporated. It will be rough like biscuit dough.

Transfer the berry mixture to a seasoned 10-inch (25-cm) cast-iron skillet using a slotted spoon, leaving behind the extra juices. Divide the dough into seven small balls about ¼ cup (55 g) in volume, flattening each slightly and placing on top of the blueberry mixture, spacing them about ½ inch (1 cm) apart. The dough should cover almost all the berries. With a pastry brush, lightly brush the tops of the biscuits with a little bit of the remaining cream. Set the skillet on a sheet pan to catch any overflowing juices and transfer it to the oven. Bake until golden on top and bubbling, 40 to 45 minutes.

While the cobbler bakes, whip the remaining cream to soft peaks by hand with a whisk or hand beaters. Sweeten it if desired, adding 8 grams (1 tbsp) of powdered sugar. Keep the cream refrigerated until ready to serve.

Remove the cobbler from the oven and allow it to cool for 10 to 15 minutes before topping with the whipped cream. Garnish with a few extra thyme leaves, if desired. Store any cobbler leftovers in glass or plastic for up to 3 days, as the acid from the berries can deteriorate the cast iron.

Malted Milk and Dark Chocolate Tart

MAKES ONE 10-INCH (25-CM) TART

Crust

94 g (¾ cup) all-purpose flour

100 g (½ cup) granulated sugar

6 g (1 tbsp) Dutch process cocoa powder

½ tsp kosher salt

57 g (4 tbsp) unsalted butter, melted

17 g (1 tbsp) discard sourdough starter

Filling

142 g (5 oz) dark chocolate, 60% to 70%, melted

114 g (1 stick) unsalted butter, melted and cooled slightly

Malt is one of those flavors most of us love but have no idea what it is. That's OK—I got you. It's a combination of pulverized barley, evaporated milk and wheat flour, processed into a very fine powder and somehow, it's crazy delicious. It was marketed in the nineteenth century as a nutritional supplement, but one day apparently a soda jerk in Chicago started adding it to chocolate shakes and the rest is history. Malt is why everything tastes better at the diner, and these days we see the mysterious ingredient popping up in various candies, ice creams and desserts—but you've probably never used it at home. The good news is it's easy to find at health food stores or in larger supermarkets, typically by the hot cocoa mixes. It goes hand in hand with sourdough and *loves* being around chocolate too. This tart hits all the spots for a sock-me-sideways dessert, and I love it so much, I added it to the menu at the restaurant, where it's a bestseller.

Heat the oven to 325ºF (165ºC) with a rack in the center. Spray a 10-inch (25-cm) springform cake pan with neutral nonstick cooking spray and set aside. To make the crust: In a mixing bowl, combine the flour, sugar, cocoa powder and salt. Mix to combine. In a separate container, mix the melted butter and discard sourdough starter. Add it to the dry ingredients, mixing with a spatula until all the dry ingredients are incorporated and the mixture is crumbly with bits ranging from pea- to marble-sized. Transfer the crumbly mixture to the prepared pan and gently press it into an even layer, covering the bottom of the pan but not going up the sides. The crust should be very lightly packed in; over-packing will make it hard to remove from the base when slicing. Refrigerate for 20 minutes.

Once chilled, place the pan on a sheet pan and bake until set and crisp, 25 to 30 minutes. Cool at room temperature.

To make the filling: Place the chocolate in a heatproof bowl and set it over a small, deep pot with about 2 inches (5 cm) of simmering water; make sure the bowl doesn't touch the water. Stir occasionally until fully melted, about 5 minutes, remove from the heat, then add the cooled, melted butter. Stir to combine. Set aside to cool for 5 minutes.

(continued)

Malted Milk and Dark Chocolate Tart (Continued)

Filling (cont.)

100 g (½ cup) granulated sugar

4 large egg yolks

1 large whole egg

28 g (2 tbsp) active sourdough starter

7 g (1 tbsp) malted milk powder

1 tsp vanilla extract

1 tsp kosher salt

Ganache

255 g (9 oz) milk chocolate, finely chopped

240 ml (1 cup) heavy cream

7 g (1 tbsp) malted milk powder

½ tsp vanilla extract

Pinch of kosher salt

28 g (2 tbsp) unsalted butter, room temperature

Cocoa powder, to garnish

Flaky sea salt, to garnish

In a mixing bowl with hand beaters or using a stand mixer with the whisk attachment, beat together the granulated sugar, egg yolks and whole egg until light and fluffy, about 3 minutes. Drizzle in the melted chocolate-and-butter mixture and beat to incorporate. Add the sourdough starter, malt powder, vanilla and salt and mix until uniform. The batter will be loose and pourable, like a brownie batter. Pour the chocolate batter into the pan with the cooled crust, smoothing it out into an even layer with the spatula. Bake until set, 20 to 25 minutes. Remove the pan from the oven and allow it to cool to room temperature.

To make the malted milk chocolate ganache: Set the milk chocolate in a deep, heatproof mixing bowl. In a small pot, combine the cream, malted milk powder, vanilla and a pinch of salt. Bring it to a boil, whisking to incorporate the malt. As soon as it starts to bubble up, remove it from the heat. Pour the cream mixture over the milk chocolate and let it sit for 5 minutes, then whisk vigorously until it comes together in a smooth, glossy ganache. Add the soft butter and whisk until fully incorporated. Cover the ganache and let it sit at room temperature to cool slightly and thicken up, about 30 minutes.

When the tart is cooled to room temperature, stir the ganache and pour it over the top, giving the pan a gentle shimmy to help spread it out into an even layer. Transfer the tart to the fridge for at least 4 hours and up to overnight.

When ready to serve, remove the tart from the fridge. Run a paring knife under very hot water. Quickly dry it off and run it around the edge of the tart to separate it from the sides of the pan. Release the ring of the springform pan and carefully remove it. Leave the tart on the base of the pan for serving and transfer it to a platter. Garnish with a light dusting of cocoa powder using a fine sieve and finish with flaky salt just before serving. Serve chilled or at room temperature.

Spiced Pear, Crème Fraîche and Almond Galette

MAKES ONE 10-INCH (25-CM) GALETTE

This freeform pie is my go-to when I need an unfussy fruit dessert. Think rustic and elegant all at once. It's relatively easy to shape and quite forgiving, even when the filling leaks out a little, which is why I recommend it to novice bakers. The dough incorporates discard, which gives the crust a sturdy, crisp bottom. The pears make this an ideal cool-weather dessert, but you could easily swap in any stone fruit in the warmer months or apples if that's what you've got on hand. I love how the fresh ginger gives it a spicy punch against the richness of the crème fraîche, and vanilla ice cream is most welcome at the party.

Crust

188 g (1½ cups) all-purpose flour, plus more for rolling

114 g (1 stick) unsalted butter, cut into ½-inch (1-cm) cubes and chilled

26 g (2 tbsp) granulated sugar

¼ tsp kosher salt

203 g (¾ cup) discard sourdough starter

30 to 45 ml (2 to 3 tbsp) cold water

Filling

4 large ripe pears (Bartlett, Anjou or Comice are my favorites)

Juice of ½ lemon

105 g (⅓ cup plus 3 tbsp) granulated sugar, divided

16 g (2 tbsp) cornstarch

15 g (2 tsp) fresh grated ginger

Seeds of ½ vanilla pod or 10 ml (2 tsp) vanilla extract

½ tsp ground cardamom

½ tsp kosher salt

To make the crust: In a mixing bowl combine the flour, cold butter cubes, sugar and salt. With your hands, work the butter into the flour, pinching it together, until it resembles a crumbly meal with pea-sized bits of butter. Add the discard sourdough starter and 15 to 30 milliliters (1 to 2 tbsp) of cold water, bringing the dough together with a spatula. It will be sticky at first as you work the starter in but then become easier to handle like a standard pie crust. It should remain slightly crumbly but hold together when you press a handful together. If it's too dry, add another 15 to 30 milliliters (1 to 2 tbsp) of water. If it's too sticky, add a little flour, no more than 8 grams (1 tbsp) at a time. Turn the dough out onto a sheet of plastic wrap, form into a disc 1 inch (2.5 cm) thick, wrap and chill for at least 1 hour and up to 24 hours.

While the dough chills, make the filling: Slice the pears in half lengthwise, removing the seeds and core; a melon baller works well for this. Slice into ⅛-inch (2.5-mm) slices. Transfer the pears to a bowl with the lemon juice and toss well to prevent oxidation. Add the 66 grams (⅓ cup) of sugar, cornstarch, ginger, vanilla seeds, cardamom and salt. Mix well. Cover and set aside to macerate at room temperature for 30 minutes to 1 hour. If you are making the pear filling ahead of time, you can refrigerate it for up to 3 hours.

(continued)

Spiced Pear, Crème Fraîche and Almond Galette

(Continued)

Filling (cont.)

120 ml (½ cup) crème fraîche

1 large egg yolk

1 large whole egg mixed with 15 ml (1 tbsp) water, for egg wash

22 g (¼ cup) sliced, raw almonds

Vanilla ice cream, for serving (optional)

In another small bowl, mix the crème fraîche and egg yolk with 26 grams (2 tbsp) of sugar until uniform. Transfer to the fridge until you're ready to assemble.

Remove the dough from the fridge and let it sit at room temperature for about 15 minutes to soften a little. Lay a large piece of parchment paper on your work surface and dust it with flour. Unwrap the dough and place it on the parchment. Gently roll it out into a 14-inch (36-cm) circle in diameter and about ¼ inch (6 mm) thick, rotating the parchment about 90 degrees every few rolls as you go to make as even a circle as you can. If the dough sticks to the rolling pin, add a little more flour. Once you have a 14-inch (36-cm) circle, use kitchen shears to trim off any particularly rough edges and even the shape out a little. Transfer the parchment with the dough to a sheet pan— it's OK if the dough hangs over the edge a little. Spread the crème fraîche mixture over the dough, leaving a 2-inch (5-cm) border.

Scoop up the pear slices by hand to drain away the liquid and arrange them on top of the crème fraîche, maintaining a 2-inch (5-cm) border of dough. Beat the egg and water together to make a wash and brush the border of the dough and then gently fold the edges over the pears in sections, creating pleats as you go. You should have seven overlapping sections, with a 1½-inch (4-cm) rustic crust all the way around. Transfer the galette to the fridge and chill for 30 minutes.

Heat the oven to 400°F (200°C) with a rack in the center. Remove the galette from the fridge and drizzle 15 milliliters (1 tbsp) of the liquid from the pears over the sliced pears. Brush the egg wash over the whole crust using your fingers or a pastry brush. Sprinkle the crust and the pears evenly with the almonds, allowing some to stick to the crust and the rest to cover the fruit. Then dust the crust with the remaining 13 grams (1 tbsp) of granulated sugar.

Bake until golden brown and bubbling, 40 to 45 minutes. Allow the galette to cool slightly before transferring to a serving platter. Slice and enjoy with some ice cream, if desired.

Walnut-Maple Black Cocoa Tart

MAKES ONE 9-INCH
(23-CM) TART

Maple and walnuts are a pairing I've always gravitated toward, with maple's intense sweetness balanced by the walnut's earthy quality. I've been making versions of this tart for years and the key is a rich, dark maple syrup—it's *got* be the real stuff. The sourdough crust is thin, crisp and flaky and balances out the super sweet, slightly boozy, soft filling. Black cocoa is dramatic stuff and it gives this tart some real moody vibes, but it's actually not nearly as acidic as standard Dutch process cocoa thanks to more processing. My favorite brand is sold by King Arthur Flour, but if you can't get your hands on some don't stress. Regular Dutch process cocoa powder will work just fine here, but expect a lighter color and a little more acidity.

Crust

94 g (¾ cup) all-purpose flour, plus more for rolling

4 g (2 tsp) black cocoa powder

26 g (2 tbsp) granulated sugar

¼ tsp kosher salt

57 g (4 tbsp) unsalted butter, cut into ½-inch (1-cm) cubes and chilled

55 g (¼ cup) active sourdough starter

30 to 45 ml (2 to 3 tbsp) cold water

To make the crust: In a mixing bowl, combine the flour, cocoa powder, sugar and salt. Add the chilled butter, and using your hands or a pastry cutter, pinch the butter into the dough until the mixture is mealy, with pea-sized bits of butter. Add the sourdough starter and 30 milliliters (2 tbsp) of water and bring the dough together by hand, adding another 15 milliliters (1 tbsp) of water if it's too crumbly. Turn the dough out onto your work surface and form into a disc. Wrap the disc of dough in plastic and refrigerate for 1 hour.

Take the dough out of the fridge and let it temper at room temperature for 10 minutes. Unwrap the dough and on a lightly floured surface, roll the disc out into a 12-inch (30-cm) circle. Transfer the dough to a 9-inch (23-cm) fluted tart pan with a removable bottom, and gently press the dough into the bottom and sides. I like to leave it rustic on top, with the dough going beyond the top of the tart pan by ½ inch (1 cm), snipping off the excess with kitchen shears. Place the pan onto a sheet pan and refrigerate for 30 minutes before baking.

Heat the oven to 350°F (177°C) with a rack in the center. Take the crust out of the fridge and line it with a piece of parchment paper, large enough to go up the sides of the pan and line the dough completely. Fill the crust with an even layer of pie weights or baking beans that fill the tart shell completely to prevent shrinking. Use about 582 grams (3 cups) of beans or weights. Transfer the pan to the oven to bake for 25 minutes. Remove it from the oven and allow it to cool at room temperature with the pie weights intact, so it doesn't shrink.

(continued)

Filling

3 large egg yolks

1 large whole egg

34 g (2 tbsp) discard sourdough starter

1 tsp black cocoa powder

240 ml (1 cup) dark maple syrup

79 ml (⅓ cup) heavy cream

57 g (4 tbsp) unsalted butter

26 g (2 tbsp) granulated sugar

15 ml (1 tbsp) bourbon

½ tsp vanilla extract

½ tsp kosher salt

117 g (1 cup) roughly chopped walnuts

Flaky sea salt, to garnish

To make the filling: Add the egg yolks, whole egg, discard sourdough starter and cocoa in a small bowl. Whisk well to combine. Set aside. In a saucepan over medium-high heat, combine the maple syrup, cream, butter, sugar, bourbon, vanilla and salt. Stir occasionally and bring the mixture to a simmer. Turn the heat to low and using a ladle, add about 120 milliliters (½ cup) of the hot liquid mixture to the egg yolk mixture and whisk well to temper. Add the egg yolk mixture back to the pot and with a spatula stir constantly until it thickens enough to coat the spatula, being careful to not overcook and curdle the mixture, 2 to 3 minutes.

When thickened, remove the custard from the heat and strain it through a fine strainer set over a bowl. Allow the mixture to cool at room temperature, about 30 minutes, before assembling the tart.

Lower the oven to 325ºF (165ºC). Remove the pie weights and parchment paper from the par-baked crust, leaving it on the sheet pan. Pour the filling into the crust and top with the walnuts. Transfer the tart to the oven and bake for about 30 minutes, until the custard is set with a slight wobble.

Remove the tart from the oven and allow it to cool at room temperature before unmolding. Carefully remove the outer ring of the pan, and garnish with flaky salt before slicing and serving.

Apple-Maple Crumble Pie

MAKES ONE 10-INCH
(25-CM) PIE

When it comes to apple pie, a crumble topping is the only way I ever want to go. There's just something about the contrast of a crunchy crumble against the soft apples and a perfectly baked bottom crust that's so satisfying. Maple sugar can be a little tricky to find but it's really worth it, especially for the topping, so see if you can get your hands on some. The farmers' market is a great place to start, as most vendors who sell the syrup also have the coveted sugar. The sourdough starter makes a very crispy, crunchy crust, which means no blind baking for this recipe and no soggy bottom!

Crust

188 g (1½ cups) all-purpose flour, plus more for rolling

114 g (1 stick) unsalted butter, cut into ½-inch (1-cm) cubes and chilled

26 g (2 tbsp) granulated sugar

¼ tsp kosher salt

147 g (⅔ cup) active sourdough starter

30 to 45 ml (2 to 3 tbsp) cold water

Crumb Topping

125 g (1 cup) all-purpose flour

100 g (½ cup) granulated sugar

40 g (¼ cup) maple sugar

½ tsp kosher salt

½ tsp ground cinnamon

57 g (4 tbsp) butter, melted and cooled slightly

55 g (3 tbsp) discard sourdough starter

To make the crust: Combine the flour, cold butter cubes, granulated sugar and salt in a mixing bowl. With your hands, work the butter into the flour, pinching it together, until it resembles a crumbly meal with pea-sized bits of butter. Add the sourdough starter, plus 30 milliliters (2 tbsp) of water, bringing the dough together with your hands. It should remain crumbly but hold together when you press a handful together. If it's too dry add another 15 to 30 milliliters (1 to 2 tbsp) of water, 15 milliliters (1 tbsp) at a time, just until the dough holds together. If it's too sticky, add a little flour, no more than 8 grams (1 tbsp) at a time. Turn the dough out onto a lightly floured work surface and press it into a rectangle about ½ inch (1 cm) thick. Fold the rectangle in half so the short sides meet up, and gently press it together so it's about 1 inch (2.5 cm) thick. Shape the dough into a disc with your hands, wrap it in plastic and transfer to the fridge to chill for at least 1 hour.

While the crust chills, make the topping: In a mixing bowl, combine the flour, granulated sugar, maple sugar, salt and cinnamon. Mix to combine. Add the butter and discard sourdough starter and mix with a spatula until no dry bits remain and the mixture is crumbly. Transfer to the fridge.

(continued)

Apple-Maple Crumble Pie
(Continued)

Filling

1.4 kg (3 lb, about 6 large) tart apples, unpeeled, cored and sliced ¼ inch (3 mm) thick

Juice of 1 lemon

57 g (4 tbsp) unsalted butter

50 g (4 tbsp) granulated sugar, divided

30 g (3 tbsp) maple sugar

1 tsp ground cinnamon

1 tsp ground ginger

¼ tsp ground cloves

¼ tsp ground cardamom

¼ tsp kosher salt

34 g (2 tbsp) discard sourdough starter

Vanilla ice cream, for serving (optional)

To make the filling: Toss the apples with the lemon juice in a bowl. In a large pot over medium heat, add the butter. When melted and bubbling, about 30 seconds, add the sliced apples and stir to coat in the butter. Add 39 grams (3 tbsp) of granulated sugar, the maple sugar, cinnamon, ginger, cloves, cardamom and salt. Gently stir to evenly distribute. Cook the mixture for 10 minutes to soften the apples, stirring occasionally, then add the sourdough starter, gently folding in to distribute. It may look clumpy at first but will soon dissolve into the juices and thicken them up. Allow the mixture to cook for another 2 to 3 minutes; it should be thick and jammy, but the apples should hold their shape. Remove from the heat and allow to cool to room temperature.

Heat the oven to 350°F (177°C) with a rack in the center. Remove the dough from the fridge and let it sit at room temperature for about 10 minutes. Unwrap the dough and on a lightly floured work surface roll it out with a rolling pin to a 14-inch (36-cm) circle, rotating the dough in 90-degree turns as you go so it doesn't stick, and lightly dusting with bench flour as needed if it feels sticky. Drape the dough over the rolling pin and transfer it to a 10-inch (25-cm) pie plate, settling it into the bottom and allowing the excess to hang over the edges. With kitchen shears, trim around the edge of the dough to even it out, leaving a 2-inch (5-cm) overhang. Tuck the overhanging dough under and into the pie plate, leaving a 1-inch (2.5-cm)-high rim of dough to crimp. Crimp as desired, using your thumbs. Transfer the crust to the fridge to chill for 20 minutes while the oven heats.

When you're ready to bake, remove the crust from the fridge and place it on a sheet pan lined with foil to catch any drips. Dust the bottom of the formed crust with the remaining 11 grams (1 tbsp) of granulated sugar. Fill the crust with the apple mixture and its syrupy juices. Remove the crumb topping from the fridge and pile it on top of the apples.

Transfer the pie to the oven and bake until golden and bubbling, 50 to 60 minutes. Remove from the oven and allow the pie to cool for at least 45 minutes before slicing. Enjoy warm or at room temperature, ideally with vanilla ice cream if desired.

Summer Fruit Marzipan Crumble

You're either a marzipan person or you're not. But if you're a marzipan freak like me, look no further. I love using marzipan paste, especially with fruit-based desserts, and it makes this crumble topping uniquely textured and decidedly almondy. Even better, you can use any mixture of summer fruits you like. But wait, there's more. This whole recipe can use discard. I'd recommend using discard that's no more than three days old and bringing it back to room temperature before incorporating it into the topping. So, marzipan lovers, you've got no reason not to make this simple showstopper in the summer when stone fruits and berries are at their peak and your sourdough starter is in full swing.

Crumble

125 g (1 cup) all-purpose flour, plus more if needed

73 g (½ cup) dark brown sugar, packed

90 g (⅓ cup) marzipan paste

36 g (⅓ cup) sliced almonds

½ tsp kosher salt

68 g (¼ cup) discard sourdough starter

57 g (4 tbsp) melted butter, cooled slightly

Filling

1.3 kg (8 cups total) summer fruit, cut into ½- to 1-inch (1- to 2.5-cm)-thick pieces (I recommend a mix of berries, pitted cherries and sliced stone fruits.)

1 tsp vanilla extract

Juice of ½ lemon

100 g (½ cup) granulated sugar

16 g (2 tbsp) cornstarch

Vanilla ice cream, for serving (optional)

To make the crumble topping: In a mixing bowl, combine the flour and brown sugar, mixing by hand to break up any clumps of brown sugar. Dust your fingers with a little additional flour, pinch off pea-sized bits of the marzipan and add them to the flour mixture. Toss to coat the marzipan and evenly distribute. Add the almonds and salt. Mix to combine evenly. Whisk the discard sourdough starter into the cooled melted butter, then add it to the dry mixture, mixing with a spatula until the mixture is crumbly. You'll have pea- to marble-sized clusters of dough. Transfer to the fridge. Heat the oven to 400°F (200°C) with a rack in the center.

To make the filling: Combine the prepared fruit with the vanilla and lemon juice in a large mixing bowl. Add the granulated sugar and gently mix to coat the fruit. Let it sit and macerate at room temperature for 20 minutes, then gently tilt the bowl, using your hands to hold the fruit, to drain the liquid, leaving about 45 milliliters (3 tbsp) behind. Toss the drained fruit with the cornstarch.

Using a slotted spoon, transfer the fruit to a 9- or 10-inch (23- or 25-cm) deep cast-iron pan, leaving the juices behind in the bowl. Top the fruit with 45 milliliters (3 tbsp) of the juices, then top with the chilled crumble in an even layer.

Transfer to the oven, placing a sheet pan below to catch any overflowing juices, and bake for 15 minutes. Lower the temperature to 350°F (177°C) and bake until bubbly and crisp on top, 30 to 35 minutes. Remove from the oven and allow the crumble to cool for 20 minutes before serving, ideally with vanilla ice cream if desired.

Blackberry-Pistachio Frangipane Tart

MAKES ONE 9-INCH (23-CM) TART

Crust

187 g (1½ cups) all-purpose flour

75 g (½ cup plus 2 tbsp) powdered sugar

½ tsp kosher salt

55 g (¼ cup) active sourdough starter

114 g (1 stick) unsalted butter, melted

Filling

75 g (a heaping ½ cup) raw shelled pistachios

114 g (1 stick) melted butter, cooled slightly

100 g (½ cup) granulated sugar

½ tsp kosher salt

2 large eggs

55 g (¼ cup) active sourdough starter

1 tsp vanilla extract

170 g (6 oz) fresh blackberries, sliced in half

1 tsp Demerara or sanding sugar (optional)

Frangipane! I love you so much! There's so much to say about this beauty, I don't even know where to begin. Frangipane is kind of like marzipan's more rustic cousin, traditionally made with ground almonds, but I've swapped in pistachios for this and it's otherworldly. The buttery sweetness of the pistachio pairs so well with the inky, earthy blackberries that bleed into the bright green filling. Sourdough works its magic in both the crust and the filling, bringing it all together with the perfect combination of sweet and sour. This recipe is pretty luxurious in its ingredients, but easy to throw together and 100% worth it.

To make the crust: Combine the flour, powdered sugar and salt in a mixing bowl. Add the sourdough starter to the melted butter and whisk to combine. Add it to the dry ingredients, mixing with a spatula to combine. It will be the consistency of a very buttery shortbread dough.

Heat the oven to 350°F (177°C) with a rack in the center. Transfer the crust mixture to a 9-inch (23-cm) nonstick fluted tart pan with a removable bottom and spread it into an even layer. Use your hands to gently pack the crust in, going fully up the sides of the pan. Place the formed crust on a sheet pan and transfer to the freezer to chill for 1 hour. Then bake until golden, 25 to 30 minutes. Allow it to cool in the pan.

To make the filling: Add the pistachios to a food processor and grind until they are the consistency of coarse sand. In a mixing bowl, whisk together the ground pistachios, cooled melted butter, granulated sugar and salt to form a paste. Add the eggs, sourdough starter and vanilla, whisking until smooth and uniform. Pour the pistachio frangipane into the prepared crust, smoothing it out into an even layer with the spatula. Dot the tart with the blackberries in a single layer, spacing them out as desired. Sprinkle the Demerara sugar evenly across the top of the tart if using, and then transfer it to the oven on the sheet pan.

Bake until set and golden brown around the edges, with a little wobble in the center, 30 to 35 minutes. The frangipane shouldn't look wet on top. Remove the tart from the oven and allow it to cool to room temperature in the pan. Once cooled, carefully remove the outer fluted ring and place the tart on a serving platter to slice.

Baked or Fried Apple-Ginger Hand Pies

A hand pie is such a brilliant thing because . . . it's a pie. That you can hold! In your hands! I love the filling of these, spiced with plenty of ginger, both fresh and ground, for extra coziness. They shine whether baked or fried, so pick your poison. Baked, they become flaky with crispy bottoms, while fried they become light and crackly with a little chew. I like to finish both with lots of powdered sugar. And while the fried ones are best enjoyed right away, the baked ones hold up for several hours.

MAKES 8 HAND PIES

Filling

28 g (2 tbsp) unsalted butter

567 g (1¼ lb) crisp, tart apples, diced into ½-inch (1-cm) cubes

55 g (¼ cup) dark brown sugar, packed

26 g (2 tbsp) granulated sugar

4 g (2 tsp) fresh grated ginger

1 tsp vanilla extract

½ tsp ground cinnamon

¼ tsp ground ginger

¼ tsp kosher salt

14 g (1 tbsp) discard sourdough starter

To make the filling: Melt the butter in a large pot over medium heat. When bubbling, add the apples and stir to coat in the butter. Add the brown sugar, granulated sugar, grated ginger, vanilla, cinnamon, ground ginger and salt. Gently mix to evenly distribute. Allow the mixture to cook down for about 20 minutes; it should be thick and jammy. Add the discard sourdough starter and fold in to evenly distribute. Cook another 2 minutes to thicken.

Remove from the heat and cool to room temperature. You can make this filling up to 3 days ahead and refrigerate.

(continued)

Baked or Fried Apple-Ginger Hand Pies (Continued)

Crust

188 g (1½ cups) all-purpose flour, plus more for rolling

114 g (1 stick) unsalted butter, cut into ½-inch (1-cm) cubes and chilled

26 g (2 tbsp) granulated sugar

¼ tsp kosher salt

147 g (⅔ cup) active sourdough starter

30 to 45 ml (2 to 3 tbsp) ice cold water

1 large egg mixed with 30 ml (2 tbsp) water, for egg wash

2 L (64 oz) canola oil, if frying

Powdered sugar, for dusting

To make the crust: Combine the flour, cold butter cubes, sugar and salt in a mixing bowl. With your hands, work the butter into the flour, pinching it together, until it resembles a crumbly meal with pea-sized bits of butter. Add the sourdough starter and water, bringing the dough together with your hands. It should remain slightly crumbly but hold together when you press a handful together. If it's too dry, add another 15 to 30 milliliters (1 to 2 tbsp) of water, 15 milliliters (1 tbsp) at a time. If it's too sticky, add a little flour 8 grams (1 tbsp) at a time.

Turn the dough out onto a lightly floured work surface and press it into a rectangle about ½ inch (1 cm) thick. Fold the rectangle in half so the short sides meet up, and gently press it together so it's about 1 inch (2.5 cm) thick. It'll be a little shaggy and messy; don't worry. Wrap the rectangle in plastic and refrigerate for at least 1 hour.

Remove the dough from the fridge. On a floured surface with a rolling pin, roll the dough out to a 12 x 9-inch (30 x 23-cm) rectangle, dusting with flour as needed if the dough feels a little sticky. Fold the short edges of the rectangle into the center, overlapping like a brochure. Then rotate the dough 90 degrees and roll it out again to a 17 x 12-inch (43 x 30-cm) rectangle. If the dough is giving you a lot of resistance and bouncing back, leave it in place, cover with a sheet of plastic and let it rest for 10 minutes before continuing to roll out.

Dust a sheet pan with flour and set aside. In a small bowl, whisk together the egg and 30 milliliters (2 tbsp) of water to make a light egg wash. Trim just the edges of the rectangle to neaten it up and then cut it into eight even 4¼ x 4¼-inch (11 x 11-cm) squares.

With a pastry brush, egg wash all the edges of each square. Using a ¼-cup (60-ml) measure, scoop a portion of the cooled filling into the center of each square, then fold it in half on the diagonal into a triangle. With a fork, press the edges together firmly. If it's sticky, dip the tines of the fork in a little flour as you go. Pierce the top of the hand pie with the tines of the fork once and transfer the finished hand pie to the sheet pan using a metal spatula. Repeat with the remaining dough until you've formed eight hand pies. Transfer the tray of hand pies to the freezer for 30 minutes.

FRIED VARIATION

Fill a large deep pot with the canola oil and clip a candy thermometer to the side. Turn the heat to medium-high and heat the oil to 350 to 360°F (177 to 182°C). While the oil heats up, set up a sheet pan with a resting rack set on top. Have a slotted spoon handy, along with a bowl of powdered sugar and a small, fine strainer.

When the oil reaches about 350°F (177°C), remove the hand pies from the freezer and very carefully lower one pie at a time into the oil, only frying two pies at a time. Allow the pies to fry until deep golden brown, about 5 minutes, flipping over halfway through. When ready, use the slotted spoon to scoop the pies out of the hot oil, one by one, and transfer to the resting rack. Repeat with the remaining pies, until they're all fried. Then dust liberally with powdered sugar and enjoy warm. Remember to turn off the oil and allow it to cool completely at room temperature before disposing.

BAKED VARIATION

Heat the oven to 350°F (177°C) with a rack in the center. After the shaped hand pies have chilled in the freezer for 30 minutes, brush each with the remaining egg wash, transfer to the oven and bake until golden and crisp, 35 to 40 minutes. Remove from the oven and allow to cool on the sheet pan for 20 minutes, then dust liberally with powdered sugar and enjoy warm.

Honey-Nut Halvah Tart

MAKES ONE 9-INCH
(23-CM) TART

Crust

156 g (1¼ cups) all-purpose flour

50 g (⅓ cup plus 1 tbsp) powdered sugar

35 g (¼ cup) rye flour

½ tsp kosher salt

68 g (¼ cup) discard sourdough starter

114 g (1 stick) unsalted butter, melted

Filling

227 g (8 oz) pistachio halvah, crumbled and divided (see Note)

129 g (1 cup) roughly chopped lightly toasted unsalted, mixed nuts (My favorite is a mixture of almonds, walnuts, hazelnuts and cashews.)

73 g (⅓ cup) active sourdough starter

2 large eggs

45 ml (3 tbsp) honey, plus 15 ml (1 tbsp) to garnish

25 g (2 tbsp) granulated sugar

30 ml (2 tbsp) whole milk

1 tsp kosher salt

Flaky sea salt, to garnish

I came up with this recipe right around the Jewish New Year as I got inspired by Rosh Hashana and the culinary symbolism of the holiday. I've always loved the food associated with that particular celebration because it's all about the sweetness. Honey appears in cakes and pastries or drizzled on apples to represent a sweet New Year, and it was always my favorite Jewish holiday growing up. I loved getting my fingers all sticky sweet after dinner on desserts like teiglach, honey cake or simple, crisp slices of apple dunked in honey. Feel free to use your favorite blend of nuts in this tart. They get combined with sourdough and a honey-and-halvah custard. I love the addition of a little rye flour in the crust, which I think has a chamomile-like aroma. It perfectly complements this gloriously sticky, nutty creation.

To make the crust: Combine the all-purpose flour, powdered sugar, rye flour and salt in a medium mixing bowl. In a separate small bowl, whisk together the discard sourdough starter and the melted butter, then add it to the dry mixture, mixing with a spatula to combine. It will be the consistency of a buttery shortbread dough.

Heat the oven to 325ºF (165ºC) with a rack in the center. Transfer the crust mixture to a 9-inch (23-cm) nonstick fluted tart pan with a removable bottom and spread it into an even layer. Use your hands to gently pack the crust in, going fully up the sides of the pan. Place the formed crust on a sheet pan and transfer to the freezer to chill for 30 minutes. Then bake until golden, about 30 minutes. Remove the crust from the oven and allow it to cool completely in the pan.

While the crust cools, make the filling: In a mixing bowl, whisk together half of the halvah, the nuts, sourdough starter, eggs, 45 milliliters (3 tbsp) of honey, the granulated sugar, milk and salt until evenly combined. Pour the filling into the baked crust and top with the remaining halvah.

Transfer the tart on the sheet pan to the oven and bake until deeply toasted on top and the filling is set, 30 to 35 minutes. Remove the tart from the oven and allow to cool in the pan. Once the tart has cooled to room temperature, remove the outer ring of the pan, drizzle with the remaining tablespoon (15 ml) of honey and garnish with flaky sea salt. Slice and serve.

Note: Halvah is a staple confection found in Middle Eastern markets, traditionally made from sesame. If you can't get your hands on pistachio halvah, any flavor will work beautifully.

COOKIES, BARS and SWEET LITTLE BITES

I remember the first time I added sourdough to a batch of cookies. The flavor and texture were a revelation, and that's really saying something since I've made A LOT of cookies in my lifetime. From that first batch, things just kind of snowballed and I haven't looked back. I've fallen head over heels for the savory undertones and the robust quality sourdough adds to all these little treats, with chew and crispiness in all the right places. I stay stocked up, and if you look in my freezer, you'll likely find three or four kinds of frozen cookie dough—minimum. Chocolate chunk, shortbreads, oatmeal . . . you name it. I just sleep better at night knowing I could throw some frozen dough on a sheet pan at any moment and have fresh cookies in 15 minutes. If you're having trouble sleeping, I recommend you do the same. And don't get me started on the sheer joy of having super fudgy frozen sourdough fig brownies (page 127) in my back pocket for late-night cravings. You may never be satisfied with a conventional one again.

Double Chocolate Chunk Cookies

MAKES ABOUT 12 LARGE OR 24 SMALL COOKIES

This is my ideal cookie: It's relatively thin, crispy on the edges and chewy in the center. The deep butterscotch-like flavor is thanks to brown butter and an overnight rest, and it has plenty of puddles of chocolate with a salty pop to finish. Chunks of chocolate are a must—and are far superior to chips—because of how the chocolate distributes throughout the cookie. The brown butter is nonnegotiable too, because it imparts an incredible flavor, but more importantly, it reduces the water content in the butter to balance out the water in the sourdough starter. Without this step you'd have a cakey cookie, and that's not my vibe. Sure, it's more work chopping up the chocolate and browning the butter and resting things overnight—I get it, I know. But there's a far greater reward at the end of it. These satisfy every chocolate chip cookie craving, and if you get in the habit of keeping frozen portions of this dough in your freezer, then my job is done here.

114 g (1 stick) unsalted butter

146 g (1 cup) dark brown sugar, packed

100 g (½ cup) granulated sugar

110 g (½ cup) active sourdough starter

1 large egg

10 ml (2 tsp) vanilla extract

78 g (½ cup plus 2 tbsp) all-purpose flour

87 g (½ cup plus 2 tbsp) bread flour

1 tsp kosher salt

½ tsp baking powder

¼ tsp baking soda

213 g (1¼ cups) chopped dark chocolate chunks, 60% to 70%, divided

213 g (1¼ cups) chopped milk chocolate chunks, divided

Flaky sea salt, to garnish (optional)

Start by browning the butter. In a small, deep pot over medium-high heat, cook the butter, whisking frequently to scrape the bottom of the pot, until it's a light honey color and little brown bits form on the bottom of the pot, 4 to 5 minutes. Turn off the heat and allow it to cool slightly for 5 minutes. You should have 85 grams (3 oz) or a scant 120 milliliters (½ cup) of brown butter. Transfer to a small bowl or container, cover and refrigerate until it is opaque and a creamy consistency, about 1 hour.

Once the butter has chilled, remove it from the fridge. In a large mixing bowl, cream together the brown butter and both sugars with a wooden spoon or hand beaters until uniform, about 3 minutes. Add the sourdough starter, egg and vanilla, mixing to fully incorporate.

Add the all-purpose flour, bread flour, salt, baking powder and baking soda. Incorporate with a spatula until mostly uniform, then add 170 grams (1 cup) of dark and 170 grams (1 cup) of milk chocolate chunks, mixing to fully incorporate, reserving 43 grams (¼ cup) of each for topping the cookies.

Scoop the dough into heaping 57-gram (2-oz) balls using a scoop or eyeballing by hand; they should be about the size of golf balls. For small cookies, scoop into 28 gram (1 oz) portions. Transfer them to a parchment-lined sheet pan. Combine the reserved chocolate chunks in a small bowl and roll each cookie in them to coat the top. Cover and refrigerate overnight.

(continued)

Double Chocolate Chunk Cookies
(Continued)

Heat the oven to 350°F (177°C) with two racks in the middle third of the oven. Remove the portioned dough from the fridge and arrange the cookies on parchment-lined sheet pans, spacing them 3 inches (8 cm) apart, with no more than eight cookies to a tray.

Transfer to the oven and bake until set and slightly golden around the edges but soft in the middle, 13 to 15 minutes. Remove from the oven and, while still hot, sprinkle each cookie with a little flaky sea salt, if desired. Bake small cookies for about 13 minutes total. Repeat with the remaining dough until all the cookies are baked. Allow them to cool for at least 10 minutes on the sheet pans before enjoying.

Note: After rolling the portioned dough in the chocolate chunks, wrap well and freeze for up to 2 weeks. The cookies can be baked directly from frozen the same way, for the full 15 minutes, although they may not spread out as much as the fresh dough.

Salted Rye-Double Chocolate Pecan Cookies

These cookies are the most indulgent ones I make. Chocolate-on-chocolate can seem like overkill—and to be honest sometimes it is—until you really need it, and then it's *just* right. These cookies are deeper than they are sweet, which helps offset the indulgent ingredients. I've made many variations of this recipe, but only recently added my sourdough starter to the mix, and I love how well it plays with two kinds of chocolate and the salty finish. Rye flour has a great nutty flavor and lots of starch that assists with the satisfying, dense texture. Dark brown sugar and melted butter help to make it fudge-like. The flaky salt at the end is *not* optional so don't even think about skipping it. Neither is the resting time since the initial dough is very wet and benefits from 24 hours in the fridge. Just do as I say, and you'll be extremely happy with these.

MAKES APPROXIMATELY 12 LARGE OR 24 SMALL COOKIES

114 g (1 stick) unsalted butter

170 g (6 oz) dark chocolate, 60% to 70%, melted

65 g (¼ cup plus 2 tbsp) rye flour

42 g (½ cup) Dutch process cocoa powder

26 g (3 tbsp plus 1 tsp) all-purpose flour

1 tsp kosher salt

¼ tsp baking soda

2 large eggs

146 g (⅔ cup) dark brown sugar, packed

137 g (½ cup plus 3 tbsp) granulated sugar

1 tsp vanilla extract

75 g (⅓ cup) active sourdough starter

Start by browning the butter. In a small, deep pot over medium-high heat, cook the butter, whisking frequently to scrape the bottom of the pot, until it's a light honey color and little brown bits start to form on the bottom of the pot, 4 to 5 minutes. Remove from the heat and allow to cool slightly. You should have 85 grams (3 oz) of butter.

Place the dark chocolate in a small heatproof bowl. Set it over a small pot with about 2 inches (5 cm) of simmering water, making sure the bowl doesn't touch the water. Stir constantly until fully melted, about 5 minutes. Remove from the double boiler and pour the brown butter over the chocolate, stirring to combine.

In a small mixing bowl, combine the rye flour, cocoa powder, all-purpose flour, salt and baking soda. Whisk to combine and break up any lumps of cocoa. Set aside.

In a large mixing bowl, whisk together the eggs, dark brown sugar and granulated sugar until the sugar is fully dissolved and the mixture is pale, about 1 minute. Gradually whisk in the brown butter chocolate mixture in two additions so it emulsifies into the eggs and sugar. Add the vanilla, followed by the sourdough starter, whisking until uniform. The mixture will be like a brownie batter at this point.

(continued)

Salted Rye-Double Chocolate Pecan Cookies
(Continued)

213 g (1½ cups) chopped milk chocolate chunks, divided

114 g (1 cup) chopped pecans

A generous sprinkling of flaky sea salt, to finish

Switch to a spatula, scraping any batter off the whisk, and gently fold in the dry mixture. When halfway combined, add 170 grams (1 cup) of milk chocolate chunks and the pecans and mix until no dry bits remain. The dough will be very soft. Cover and transfer to the fridge overnight.

Heat the oven to 350°F (177°C) with two racks in the middle third of the oven. Line two sheet pans with parchment paper. Remove the dough from the fridge and let it sit at room temperature until easily scoopable, about 30 minutes. Portion the dough into 57-gram (2-oz) portions using a scoop or eyeball it; they should be about the size of a golf ball. For small cookies, scoop into 28 gram (1 oz) portions. Arrange the portioned cookie dough on the prepared pans, spacing them 3 inches (8 cm) apart, with eight cookies to a tray. Press a few chunks of the reserved milk chocolate on top of each cookie.

Transfer to the oven and bake until set, 12 to 15 minutes. Small cookies will bake for about 12 to 13 minutes. Remove from the oven and, while still hot, sprinkle each cookie with a generous pinch of flaky sea salt. Allow them to cool completely on the sheet pans before enjoying.

Note: Wrap well and freeze the balls of portioned dough, after pressing in the milk chocolate, for up to 2 weeks. The cookies can be baked directly from frozen the same way, baking for the full 15 minutes, although they may not spread out as much as the fresh dough.

Cardamom and Lemon Oatmeal Lace Cookies

MAKES 24 COOKIES

Oatmeal lace cookies are one of those things I remember from childhood but then forgot about for about 25 years, until I whipped these up and wondered why I ever forgot about them in the first place. They come together in minutes, and although they do benefit from some resting time, are almost effortless to make. For a little something extra, I loaded them up with freshly cracked black pepper, cardamom and lemon zest, which mingle together for an almost floral spice. Light, crispy and bright, they make a perfect afternoon cookie. Don't be alarmed by the looseness of the batter either. You did it right, and they'll bake off perfectly crispy and delicate!

114 g (1 stick) unsalted butter, melted

146 g (1 cup) dark brown sugar, packed

28 g (2 tbsp) active sourdough starter

1 large egg

1 tsp vanilla extract

Zest of 1 lemon

158 g (1¾ cups) rolled oats

1 tsp kosher salt

1 tsp ground cardamom

½ tsp fresh cracked black pepper

In a large mixing bowl, combine the melted butter and dark brown sugar. Whisk well to break up the brown sugar until no lumps remain. Whisk in the sourdough starter, egg, vanilla and lemon zest. Finally, add the oats, salt, cardamom and black pepper, mixing until uniform. Cover and let the mixture sit at room temperature for 30 minutes to 1 hour.

Heat the oven to 325°F (165°C) with two racks in the middle third of the oven. Line two sheet pans with parchment paper or silicone baking mats. Scoop 15-gram (1-tbsp) portions of the batter onto the sheet pans and press them out into 2-inch (5-cm) circles with your fingers or the back of the measuring spoon. Space the cookies about 2 inches (5 cm) apart.

Transfer to the oven and bake until deeply caramelized and crisp, 15 to 20 minutes. Allow them to cool on the pans until they can easily be transferred to a plate with a small offset spatula or butter knife. Repeat with any remaining batter until all the cookies are baked. Store extra cookies in an airtight container at room temperature for up to 5 days.

Hazelnut, White Chocolate and Rosemary Shortbread

MAKES ABOUT 20 COOKIES

228 g (2 sticks) unsalted butter, softened at room temperature, divided

80 g (⅔ cup) powdered sugar

110 g (½ cup) active sourdough starter

2 tsp vanilla extract

300 g (2⅓ cups plus 1 tbsp) all-purpose flour, plus more for shaping as needed

2 g (1 tbsp) finely chopped rosemary, from 1 large sprig

1 tsp kosher salt

86 g (¾ cup) chopped, roasted, peeled hazelnuts

85 g (½ cup) chopped white chocolate chunks

Shortbread is the simplest, most perfect cookie. Butter, sugar, flour and salt gets you there conventionally, but since I can't help myself, I worked out a sourdough version. Rosemary may seem a little out of left field, but trust me, it's absolutely incredible and aromatic. Its savory nature is tempered by the sweet, buttery white chocolate and it goes hand in hand with the hazelnuts. This is a rich, wintery cookie, softened a bit by the addition of sourdough starter. I'm known for keeping a stash of it chilled, ready to slice and bake all season long.

Start by browning the butter. In a small, deep pot over medium-high heat, cook 114 grams (1 stick) of butter, whisking frequently to scrape the bottom of the pot, until it's a deep honey color and little brown bits form on the bottom of the pot, 4 to 5 minutes. Turn off the heat and allow it to cool in the pot until the solids are a deep brown, about 1 more minute, taking care that they don't burn. Transfer to a bowl to cool completely and solidify at room temperature. This usually takes about 4 hours, so feel free to brown the butter ahead of time. It should yield 85 grams (3 oz) of brown butter and be the same creamy consistency as the room temperature butter before mixing the dough.

When the brown butter is ready, in a mixing bowl cream together the remaining 114 grams (1 stick) of room temperature butter and the brown butter with a wooden spoon or hand beaters. You can also use a stand mixer with the paddle attachment. The mixture should be uniform and smooth. Add the powdered sugar, sourdough starter and vanilla. Mix until fully combined, making sure there are no lumps of powdered sugar.

Add the all-purpose flour, rosemary and salt. Switch to a spatula, gently folding together until mostly combined, and then add the hazelnuts and white chocolate chunks, mixing to fully incorporate.

(continued)

Hazelnut, White Chocolate and Rosemary Shortbread
(Continued)

55 g (¼ cup) Demerara or coarse sanding sugar

Cover your work surface with a large piece of plastic wrap and turn the dough out onto it. Using your hands, form the dough into a log about 2½ inches (6 cm) in diameter and 12 inches (30 cm) long. The log doesn't have to be perfect and you can dust your hands with a little flour if it's sticky. Wrap it in the plastic and roll it back and forth a few times on the countertop to smooth into a cylinder. Transfer to the fridge to chill at least 4 hours or up to overnight. To avoid a flat side on the roll of dough, after the first 20 minutes of chilling, you can take it out and give it a quick reshaping to even out the sides, but I tend not to sweat it.

When ready to bake, heat the oven to 325°F (165°C) with two racks in the middle third of the oven. Line two sheet pans with parchment paper and set aside. Take the dough out of the fridge and let it sit at room temperature to soften slightly so it slices with ease, about 15 minutes. Dust your work surface evenly with the Demerara sugar and roll the log of dough back and forth over it to coat the outside in a layer of sugar. With a sharp knife cut ½-inch (1-cm)-thick slices and place them on the sheet pans, spaced about 2 inches (5 cm) apart. These cookies don't spread out much when baked, and you can fit eight to ten cookies on a sheet pan.

Bake until just golden on the edges but still pale in the centers, 15 to 20 minutes. Allow to cool for at least 10 minutes on the sheet pans before enjoying.

Millionaire Rye Shortbread Bars with Whiskey Toffee

Major confession time. I went to university in Scotland, which is where I discovered millionaire shortbread bars. They're quite common there and the local supermarket sold a packaged version that I quickly became obsessed with. One afternoon, I bought a package and could not stop myself from eating bar after bar as I studied. The only self-control I could muster was to throw the second half of the package in the trash to stop myself. A few hours, and several pub drinks, later, I found myself retrieving the bars out of the trash and finishing them off. *In my defense*, there was nothing gross in this trash can, and it held nothing but wastepaper. That was not one of my proudest moments and is some real baggage, but it's my inspiration for these bars. So maybe my little dumpster diving has an upside.

MAKES 16 BARS

Crust

114 g (1 stick) unsalted butter, softened at room temperature

50 g (⅓ cup plus 1 tbsp) powdered sugar, sifted

73 g (⅓ cup) active sourdough starter

½ tsp vanilla extract

125 g (1 cup) all-purpose flour

36 g (¼ cup) rye flour

1 tsp kosher salt

Toffee

397 g (14-oz can) sweetened condensed milk

114 g (1 stick) unsalted butter

30 ml (2 tbsp) honey

60 g (¼ cup) dark brown sugar, packed

45 ml (3 tbsp) Scotch whiskey, divided

1 tsp vanilla extract

1 tsp kosher salt

Line a 9 x 9-inch (23 x 23-cm) pan with parchment paper, leaving a 2-inch (5-cm) overhang on two opposite sides. Set aside. To make the crust: In a mixing bowl, combine the butter and powdered sugar. Mix until smooth using a stiff spatula or hand beaters. Add the sourdough starter and vanilla and mix to combine. Last add the all-purpose flour, rye flour and salt, gently folding together to incorporate, with no dry bits remaining. Transfer the dough to the prepared pan and press it out into an even layer with your hands. If it's a little sticky, lightly dust your hands with flour. Once the crust is fully packed, refrigerate for 20 minutes.

Heat the oven to 350°F (177°C) with a rack in the center. Bake the chilled crust until set and golden around the edges, 30 minutes. Remove from the oven and allow it to cool to room temperature.

While the crust cools, make the toffee filling: In a small pot fitted with a candy thermometer, combine the sweetened condensed milk, butter, honey, brown sugar, 15 milliliters (1 tbsp) of whiskey, vanilla and salt. Heat over medium-high heat, whisking constantly until the mixture thickens, turns a light, milky coffee color and reads 220°F (104°C) on the candy thermometer, 8 to 10 minutes. Be sure to whisk constantly to prevent scorching on the bottom. Turn off the heat and vigorously whisk in the remaining 30 milliliters (2 tbsp) of whiskey. The mixture may bubble up and look broken for a minute, but don't worry, keep whisking until it smooths out! Working quickly, pour the toffee onto the cooled crust and smooth it out into an even layer. Allow the toffee to set at room temperature for 30 minutes before transferring to the fridge for 1 hour.

(continued)

Millionaire Rye Shortbread Bars with Whiskey Toffee
(Continued)

Ganache

255 g (9 oz) dark chocolate, 60% to 70%

240 ml (1 cup) heavy cream

1 tsp vanilla extract

¼ tsp kosher salt

14 g (1 tbsp) unsalted butter, room temperature

Flaky sea salt, to garnish

While the toffee sets, make the ganache topping: Place the chocolate in a heatproof mixing bowl. In a small pot, bring the cream and vanilla to a boil. Pour it over the chocolate, add the salt and let the mixture sit undisturbed for 5 minutes. Add the butter and whisk vigorously until smooth and then pour the ganache over the set toffee, smoothing it out into an even layer with a spatula or offset spatula. Transfer the pan to the fridge to set, uncovered, for at least 4 hours.

To unmold and slice, run a paring knife along the edges of the pan to release the bars, and then use the overhanging parchment to lift the bar out in one piece. Place on a cutting board and slice the square in half, creating two rectangles. Slice each rectangle into eight 1-inch (2.5-cm) bars, wiping the knife clean with a hot, damp towel between each slice. Finish each bar with a sprinkle of flaky salt before enjoying.

Chewy Coconut-Cashew Bars

MAKES ONE 9 X 9–INCH (23 X 23–CM) PAN

Crust

156 g (1¼ cups) all-purpose flour

110 g (½ cup) dark brown sugar, packed

¾ tsp kosher salt

86 g (6 tbsp) unsalted butter, melted

57 g (3 tbsp plus 1 tsp) discard sourdough starter

Filling

110 g (½ cup) dark brown sugar, packed

2 large eggs

57 g (¼ cup) active sourdough starter

120 ml (½ cup) sweetened condensed milk

1 tsp vanilla extract

129 g (1 cup) chopped, roasted cashews

170 g (1 cup) dark chocolate, 60% to 70%, finely chopped

87 g (¾ cup plus 3 tbsp) shredded, sweetened coconut, divided

½ tsp kosher salt

Coconut and cashew is an all-time favorite combination for me. Add chocolate and I'm set for life. I adapted this recipe from a non-sourdough version I've been making for years, because . . . why not? The brown sugar shortbread crust against a sweetened condensed milk–laced filling really benefits from a little sourdough in the mix to bring it all back down to earth. The bar shape is fun to snack on, and these keep for up to 5 days, wrapped well, at room temperature. You'll easily nosh your way through the whole batch in no time.

Heat the oven to 350°F (177°C) with a rack in the center. Line a 9 x 9-inch (23 x 23-cm) metal pan with parchment paper, leaving a 2-inch (5-cm) overhang on two opposite sides. Spray it with neutral nonstick cooking spray and set aside.

To make the crust: In a mixing bowl combine the flour, brown sugar and salt, mixing to combine. Whisk together the melted butter and discard sourdough starter, then add it to the flour mixture, mixing with a spatula or clean hands until no dry bit remains. Transfer the mixture to the prepared pan and press it out using your hands or the bottom of a drinking glass to get an even layer covering the whole bottom. Refrigerate for 20 minutes, then bake until set and just golden on the edges, 20 to 25 minutes. Remove the crust from the oven and set aside to cool.

While the crust cools, make the filling: Reduce the oven to 325°F (165°C). In a mixing bowl, whisk together the brown sugar and eggs until smooth. Add the sourdough starter, sweetened condensed milk and vanilla. Whisk until uniform. Add the cashews, dark chocolate, 70 grams (¾ cup) of coconut and salt. Mix to evenly distribute with a spatula. Pour the filling on top of the baked crust and top with the remaining 17 grams (3 tbsp) of coconut. Bake until the coconut is golden and the filling is set, 30 to 35 minutes.

Remove from the oven and allow to cool completely in the pan. Use the overhanging parchment paper to remove the bar from the pan and transfer them to a cutting board. Slice the square in half, into two rectangles, then slice the rectangles into 6 long bars each. They will keep for up to 5 days at room temperature in an airtight container.

Lemon Meringue Oat Bars

MAKES 9 TO 12 BARS

I've always adored lemon bars for their bright, puckery quality that makes my mouth water, and as it happens, they were one of the first sweets I remember baking as a little girl out of one of my kid-friendly cookbooks. These are a cross between a lemon bar and lemon meringue pie with the addition of a sturdy, buttery sourdough and oat crust, because it's my book and I can do what I want. The fluffy toasted meringue topping is such a good time, and if you've never used a blowtorch before, I highly recommend taking this opportunity to add one to your kitchen. The broiler will do in a pinch. Pucker up!

Crust

110 g (½ cup) dark brown sugar, packed

55 g (¼ cup) active sourdough starter, 100% hydration (page 11)

114 g (1 stick) unsalted butter, melted

½ tsp kosher salt

125 g (1 cup) all-purpose flour

100 g (1 cup) rolled oats

Filling

226 g (1 cup plus 2 tbsp) granulated sugar

240 ml (1 cup) strained lemon juice (from about 4 lemons)

4 large whole eggs

4 large egg yolks (reserve 2 of the whites for the meringue topping)

Zest of 4 lemons

½ tsp kosher salt

114 g (1 stick) unsalted butter, at room temperature

Heat the oven to 350°F (177°C) with a rack in the center. Lightly spray a 9 x 9-inch (23 x 23-cm) metal cake pan with a neutral nonstick cooking spray. Line the pan with a rectangle of parchment paper, leaving a 2-inch (5-cm) overhang.

To make the crust: In a mixing bowl, combine the dark brown sugar, sourdough starter, melted butter and salt, whisking to combine. Add the all-purpose flour and oats and fold in with a spatula. Transfer the mixture to the pan and with your hands press it into the bottom in an even layer, smoothing out the top as much as possible. Refrigerate for 30 minutes.

Bake the crust until browned and set, 20 to 25 minutes. Remove, turn the oven down to 300°F (149°C) and allow to cool to room temperature.

While the crust bakes, start the lemon curd filling: Fill a small pot with about 3 inches (8 cm) of water and bring to a simmer. Set a fine strainer over a nonreactive bowl; use glass or stainless steel. Set aside. In another nonreactive mixing bowl, combine the granulated sugar, lemon juice, whole eggs, yolks, lemon zest and salt. Whisk well to combine and then set the bowl over the simmering water, making sure the bottom of the bowl does not come into contact with the water. Cook, whisking constantly until the mixture starts to thicken and it coats the wires of the whisk, about 8 minutes. Add the butter 28 grams (2 tbsp) at a time, whisking to incorporate with each addition. Once all the butter is incorporated, pour the filling through the mesh strainer, and then pour the curd into the baked, cooled crust.

Transfer to the oven and bake until it's almost fully set with just a little wobble in the center, 20 to 25 minutes. Remove from the oven and let it cool fully to room temperature before transferring to the fridge for at least 4 hours or up to overnight.

Meringue Topping

100 g (½ cup) granulated sugar

2 large egg whites

Pinch of kosher salt

When the filling is fully cooled, use a small offset spatula and the overhanging parchment to carefully lift and remove the bar from the pan in one piece. Place the square on a cutting board and gently pull the parchment paper out from underneath and discard it.

To make the toasted meringue topping: Combine the sugar and egg whites in a heatproof mixing bowl and place it over a medium saucepan filled with about 3 inches (8 cm) of water. Make sure the bottom of the bowl doesn't touch the water. Allow the water to simmer while you constantly stir the egg whites and sugar with a spatula. After 8 minutes the mixture should be frothy, and the sugar should be fully dissolved. Run a little bit of the mixture between your fingers to test—if it feels a little grainy, keep going. When the sugar is fully dissolved, whip the mixture on high with hand beaters until stiff, glossy peaks form, about 5 minutes. Add a pinch of salt and whip 1 more minute.

Transfer the meringue to the lemon bars using a spatula. Smooth it out into swooshes, swirls and peaks as desired and then gently toast it with a culinary blow torch. Alternatively, place under the broiler for no more than 1 minute, watching closely so it toasts but doesn't burn. With a sharp knife, cut into squares, wiping the knife clean with a damp towel between each slice. Enjoy at room temperature or chilled.

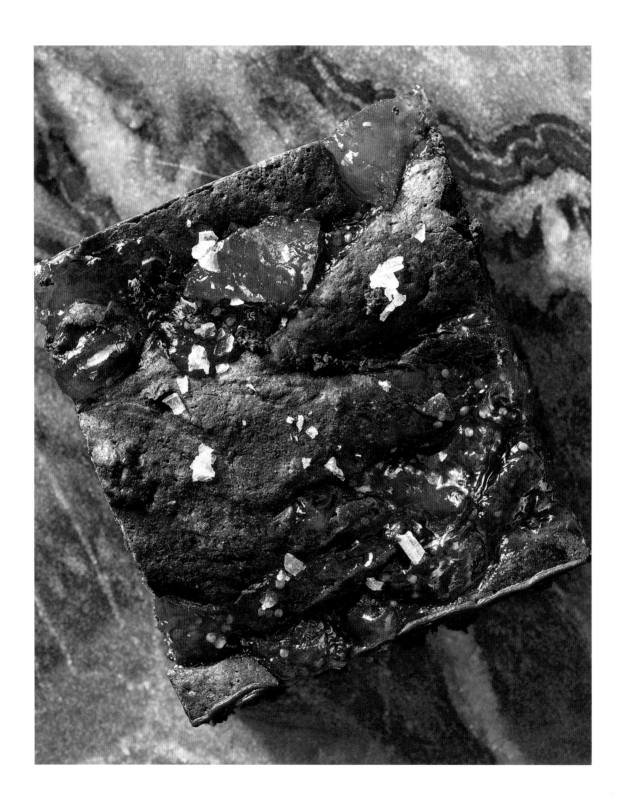

Fig-Dark Chocolate Brownies

MAKES 9 TO 12 BROWNIES

368 g (13 oz) dark chocolate, 60% to 70%

114 g (1 stick) unsalted butter

1 tsp vanilla extract

44 g (½ cup) Dutch process cocoa powder

8 g (1 tbsp) all-purpose flour

1 tsp kosher salt

4 large eggs

146 g (⅔ cup) dark brown sugar, packed

100 g (½ cup) granulated sugar

110 g (½ cup) active sourdough starter

240 ml (1 cup) fig jam

Flaky sea salt, to garnish

Fig and chocolate are another forever favorite combination of mine. When I was promoted to my first pastry chef position, a chocolate and fig tart was one of the first desserts I added to the menu, and to this day, it's one of the dishes I'm most proud of. There's something about the musky honey sweetness of the figs that brings out the fruity undertones of dark chocolate, and I always love it paired with sourdough. These brownies are rich, deep and fudgy . . . just how I like them.

Heat the oven to 325°F (165°C) with a rack in the center. Spray a 9 x 9-inch (23 x 23-cm) square pan with a neutral nonstick cooking spray, and line with a rectangle of parchment paper, leaving a 2-inch (5-cm) overhang on two opposite sides. Set aside.

Place the chocolate, butter and vanilla in a heatproof mixing bowl. Set the bowl on top of a small pot with about 2 inches (5 cm) of simmering water, making sure the bottom of the bowl does not touch the water. Stir to melt together, about 3 minutes. Remove from the heat and set aside.

In a mixing bowl, combine the cocoa powder, flour and salt. Whisk to fully combine and break up any lumps. Set aside.

In another mixing bowl, with hand beaters or a whisk, beat the eggs and both sugars until light and doubled in volume. Add the sourdough starter and mix to fully combine. Then add the chocolate mixture, and whisk or beat in until thick and uniform.

Add the dry ingredients to the chocolate mixture, switch to a spatula and fold together until no dry patches remain. Transfer the batter to the prepared pan, spreading it out into an even layer with the spatula.

Dot the top of the brownies all over with the jam and then swirl it through the batter by running a toothpick or the tip of a paring knife through the dots in any pattern you desire. Bake the brownies until set, 35 to 40 minutes. Remove from the oven, sprinkle with flaky sea salt, and allow them to cool in the pan for at least 1 hour. Use the overhanging parchment paper to lift them out of the pan and slice into squares.

CLEVER CAKES

Cakes have always been a huge part of my identity as a pastry chef. I built a following with my dramatic layered affairs featuring swoops of smooth buttercream and whimsical decorations. But I've recently found myself comfortably settling into more casual, everyday cakes, especially when baking at home—and the addition of sourdough is a newfound passion. The tangy-sweet balance makes them perfect for snacking, and despite my love for more elaborate cakes, an approachable batter that doesn't require me to lug my mixer out has become my pastry paramour. It's very liberating to just dump things into a bowl, then a pan and just bake. These cakes are simple, and you can rustle one up on a whim if you're so inclined, with added starter for a fluffy, tender crumb every time.

Apple-Sour Cream Crumb Cake

MAKES ONE 9-INCH (23-CM) CAKE

Crumb Topping

125 g (1 cup) all-purpose flour

150 g (¾ cup) granulated sugar

½ tsp ground cinnamon

½ tsp kosher salt

55 g (3 tbsp plus 1 tsp) discard sourdough starter

57 g (4 tbsp) unsalted butter, melted

Cake

2 large tart apples, such as Granny Smith, unpeeled and chopped into ½-inch (1-cm) cubes

Juice of ½ lemon

My brother George doesn't like dessert. And not like one of those people that claims to not have a sweet tooth but then rudely eats half of the sundae you ordered for yourself. He truly doesn't crave sugar and never has. Clearly, I do not have this gene, but it was of great benefit to me growing up since it meant never having to share my dessert with a sibling. There are only a handful of sweet things I can remember him ever enjoying, and a dense sour cream crumb cake was one of them. Occasionally, my mom's friend would bring over the most incredible apple–sour cream crumb cake from Balducci's, the sadly long-gone, specialty market in Manhattan's Greenwich Village. It was *so good*—the kind of cake that could even entice someone so decidedly not a dessert person, like my brother, and one of the few sweet things the two of us enjoyed equally. I've always wanted to re-create it—and with sourdough no less. It's almost equal parts apples and batter, with a generous layer of crispy streusel. Don't skimp on the obscene amount of powdered sugar at the end. It's part of the whole experience. This might be my favorite recipe in the whole book.

To make the crumb topping: In a large mixing bowl, combine the all-purpose flour, granulated sugar, cinnamon and salt. Whisk to combine and distribute everything evenly. In a separate bowl, whisk together the discard sourdough starter and melted butter. Add it to the dry ingredients, mixing with a spatula until all the dry ingredients are incorporated and the mixture is crumbly with bits ranging from pea- to marble-sized. Refrigerate until ready to use.

To make the cake: Heat the oven to 325ºF (165ºC) with a rack in the center. Spray a 10-inch (25-cm) springform cake pan with neutral nonstick cooking spray and set aside. In a large bowl, combine the chopped apples with the lemon juice, toss to coat evenly and set aside.

(continued)

Apple-Sour Cream Crumb Cake (Continued)

Cake (cont.)

114 g (1 stick) unsalted butter

200 g (1 cup) granulated sugar

1 large egg

1 tsp vanilla extract

125 g (1 cup) all-purpose flour

1 tsp kosher salt

1 tsp baking powder

1 tsp ground cinnamon

¼ tsp baking soda

165 g (¾ cup) active sourdough starter

120 ml (½ cup) sour cream, at room temperature

24 to 32 g (3 to 4 tbsp) powdered sugar, to garnish

In another mixing bowl, using a wooden spoon or hand beaters, cream the butter and granulated sugar until light and fluffy, 2 to 4 minutes. Add the egg and vanilla. Mix to combine. Add the flour, salt, baking powder, cinnamon and baking soda and gently fold together with a spatula, until no dry patches remain. The batter will be very thick and stiff. With a spatula, gently fold in the sourdough starter until it's evenly distributed. Add the apples and sour cream, gently folding through to distribute evenly. A few streaks of sour cream are OK; it's more important not to overmix this batter.

Transfer the batter to the prepared pan, using the spatula to smooth it out into an even layer. Top the cake with all the streusel. Bake until golden brown on top, set in the center and a cake tester or toothpick comes out clean, 60 to 70 minutes. Allow it to cool to room temperature. Before serving, remove the outer ring of the pan and dust the cake liberally with the powdered sugar using a small, fine strainer.

Espresso-Chocolate Bundt Cake with Salted Caramel Glaze

I'm certainly not the first person to incorporate sourdough into sweet baked goods. There's a recipe for a chocolate sourdough cake in a 1970s edition of *The Joy of Cooking* I came across while working on this book, and obviously I had to make it immediately. It's *so* simple and perfect, with incredibly concise instructions and very little detail or description, as is the style of those classic books. And it inspired me to make my own sourdough chocolate cake recipe that incorporated more of my favorite flavors. I played with my own renditions, riffing on a non-sourdough recipe I've had in my back pocket for a while, and adding some coffee and a caramel espresso glaze for a real bonus. This cake pushes all my buttons and a Bundt is just so pretty. Make sure it's fully cooled before glazing.

MAKES ONE 10-INCH (25-CM) BUNDT CAKE

Cake

250 g (2 cups) all-purpose flour

300 g (1½ cups) granulated sugar

44 g (½ cup) Dutch process cocoa powder, sifted

5 g (1 tbsp) instant espresso powder

1 tsp kosher salt

½ tsp baking soda

220 g (1 cup) active sourdough starter

240 ml (1 cup) water

120 ml (½ cup) buttermilk

120 ml (½ cup) grapeseed or canola oil

10 ml (2 tsp) vanilla extract

To make the cake: Heat the oven to 325°F (165°C) with a rack in the center. Generously spray a 10-inch (25-cm) Bundt pan with neutral nonstick cooking spray and set aside. In a large mixing bowl, whisk together the all-purpose flour, granulated sugar, cocoa powder, instant espresso powder, salt and baking soda until the mixture is uniform. Set aside. In another mixing bowl, combine the sourdough starter, water, buttermilk, oil and vanilla. Whisk to combine.

Add the wet ingredients to the dry, using a spatula to fold everything together gently, until no dry bits remain. Transfer the batter to the pan and smooth out into an even layer. Bake until set and a cake tester or toothpick comes out clean or with a few moist crumbs, 40 to 45 minutes. Remove the cake from the oven and allow to cool in the pan for 10 minutes before inverting onto a serving platter to cool completely.

(continued)

Espresso-Chocolate Bundt Cake with Salted Caramel Glaze (Continued)

Glaze

120 ml (½ cup) heavy cream

14 g (1 tbsp) unsalted butter

100 g (½ cup) granulated sugar

120 ml (½ cup) water

1 tsp kosher salt

3 g (2 tsp) instant espresso powder

30 g (¼ cup) powdered sugar, sifted

Flaky sea salt, to garnish

To make the glaze: Combine the cream and butter in a small pot. Heat to scalding. When the mixture begins to steam and you notice a few bubbles, about 5 minutes, turn off the heat and set aside.

In a second small, deep pot, combine the granulated sugar and water. It should be the texture of wet sand with no sugar crystals remaining on the sides of the pot. Over high heat, cook the sugar to a light, honey-colored caramel, about 10 minutes. If you're new to caramel, you can use a candy thermometer. Watch it closely as once the sugar is fully dissolved, it will turn from clear syrup to caramel quickly. Do not stir the sugar and water until you see it start to change color, as I find this can cause crystallization.

When you see the first signs of caramelization, carefully swirl the syrup around in the pan a few times so it colors evenly. Once it takes on a honey hue and reads 355 to 360°F (179 to 182°C) on a thermometer, reduce the heat to low and carefully pour in the heated dairy mixture, stirring to fully incorporate. Add the salt and espresso powder and whisk well, simmering for 1 minute. Turn off the heat and add the powdered sugar, whisking until smooth.

Pour the glaze over the top of the cooled cake, letting it drip down the sides. Garnish with a little flaky sea salt and allow the glaze to set for 10 minutes before slicing.

Blood Orange– Hazelnut Crumb Cake

I love all the textures going on in this cake: The topping is full of crunchy sourdough streusel morsels and pops of chopped hazelnuts; the cake is super moist beneath and studded with juicy bits of citrus and more nuts for good measure. I've always loved the aroma of hazelnuts with the floral sweetness of blood oranges, so it's worth seeking them out for this cake, but other orange varieties will work too. It's a bright, unique cake that pairs perfectly with an afternoon coffee.

MAKES ONE 10-INCH (25-CM) CAKE

Crumb Topping

94 g (¾ cup) all-purpose flour

58 g (½ cup) chopped, roasted hazelnuts

67 g (⅓ cup) granulated sugar

½ tsp kosher salt

½ tsp ground cardamom

57 g (4 tbsp) unsalted butter, melted

77 g (¼ cup) discard sourdough starter

Cake

3 medium blood oranges

200 g (1 cup) granulated sugar

114 g (1 stick) unsalted butter, softened at room temperature

110 g (½ cup) active sourdough starter

1 large egg

1 tsp vanilla extract

To make the crumb topping: In a mixing bowl, combine the all-purpose flour, hazelnuts, sugar, salt and cardamom. With a spatula, mix until uniform. In a separate small bowl, whisk together the melted butter and discard sourdough starter, then mix it gently until the mixture is crumbly, but all the dry ingredients are incorporated. Refrigerate until ready to use.

To make the cake: Before mixing the cake, heat the oven to 325°F (165°C) with a rack in the center. Generously spray a 10-inch (25-cm) springform cake pan with neutral nonstick cooking spray. Set aside.

Zest the blood oranges into a large mixing bowl and set aside. Using a paring knife, trim off the top and bottom of each orange so it sits securely on your cutting board. Run the knife down the sides of each orange to remove the peel and pith, leaving as much of the flesh as possible. Then remove the segments from the membranes and discard any seeds. The segments don't have to be perfect since they're going into the batter. Set them aside.

In the mixing bowl with the zest, add the sugar and butter, beating them together with a wooden spoon, stiff spatula or hand beaters. Add the active sourdough starter, egg and vanilla. Mix to combine.

(continued)

Blood Orange–Hazelnut Crumb Cake (Continued)

Cake (cont.)

125 g (1 cup) all-purpose flour

86 g (¾ cup) chopped, roasted hazelnuts

½ tsp kosher salt

½ tsp baking powder

¼ tsp baking soda

Powdered sugar, for dusting

Add the flour, hazelnuts, salt, baking powder and baking soda and gently fold together until just combined. Add the orange segments, folding them to distribute throughout the batter.

Transfer the batter to the prepared pan, smoothing out into an even layer. Top with the crumb topping. Bake until set and a cake tester comes out clean, 60 to 70 minutes. Cool completely in the pan before removing the outer ring, dusting liberally with powdered sugar and slicing.

Walnut-Coconut Carrot Cake

MAKES ONE 8-INCH (20-CM) THREE-LAYER CAKE OR 24 CUPCAKES

Carrot cake with cream cheese frosting is a nostalgic comfort for me. I've always made mine with walnuts and coconut, never raisins—and that's the right way to do it. We can argue about it if you're so inclined, but I know I'm right. Sourdough starter gives the batter a supple crumb structure, but holds up all the textured elements. For a slight twist, the cream cheese frosting uses a hefty portion of dark brown sugar, which gives it a deeper, nuanced sweetness, and it's lifted by a little fresh lemon. This is the only layer cake in the book, so it's perfect for a celebration, but if that feels like too much commitment, it works just as well as cupcakes. Enjoy it either way.

Cake

95 g (¾ cup) all-purpose flour

7 g (1½ tsp) baking powder

7 g (1½ tsp) baking soda

4 g (1½ tsp) ground cinnamon

4 g (1½ tsp) kosher salt

¾ tsp ground cardamom

¾ tsp ground ginger

150 g (1½ cups) carrots, peeled and grated (from 2 or 3 medium carrots)

176 g (1½ cups) finely chopped toasted walnuts

80 g (¾ cup) sweetened, shredded coconut flakes

300 g (1½ cups) granulated sugar

3 large eggs

180 ml (¾ cup) grapeseed or canola oil

165 g (¾ cup) active sourdough starter

8 ml (1½ tsp) vanilla extract

Heat the oven to 325ºF (165ºC) with a rack in the center. Line three 8-inch (20-cm) cake pans with circles of parchment paper and spray with neutral nonstick cooking spray. Alternatively, line two 12-cavity muffin tins with papers. Set aside.

To make the cake: Combine the flour, baking powder, baking soda, cinnamon, salt, cardamom and ginger in a large mixing bowl. Mix to evenly combine and then add the carrots, walnuts and coconut, making sure the carrots are fully coated in the flour. Set aside. In another large mixing bowl, combine the sugar and eggs. Whisk well until just combined. Whisking constantly, drizzle in the oil in two additions, making sure each addition is fully emulsified. Add the sourdough starter and vanilla and gently mix to combine.

Add the dry mixture to the wet, using a spatula to gently fold it together, until the mixture is uniform and no dry patches remain.

(continued)

Walnut-Coconut Carrot Cake (Continued)

Frosting

285 g (2½ sticks) unsalted butter, room temperature

155 g (¾ cup) dark brown sugar, packed

283 g (10 oz) cream cheese, room temperature

120 g (1 cup) powdered sugar

Zest of 2 lemons

20 ml (1 tbsp plus 1 tsp) lemon juice

6 ml (1¼ tsp) vanilla extract

¾ tsp kosher salt

Sweetened shredded coconut flakes, to garnish

Toasted walnuts, to garnish

Divide the batter evenly between the prepared cake pans, about 430 grams (15 oz) per pan. Smooth into an even layer. If making cupcakes, use a ¼-cup (60-ml) measure to distribute the batter evenly in the muffin tins so that it comes two-thirds of the way up the cupcake liners. Bake until light brown on top, set in the center and a cake tester or toothpick comes out clean, 25 to 30 minutes, and 30 to 35 minutes for cupcakes. Remove from the oven and allow to cool completely while you make the frosting.

To make the frosting: If you have a mixer with a paddle attachment or hand beaters, they're welcome here. If not, some elbow grease will do. In a mixing bowl, combine the butter and brown sugar. Beat on high until very light and fluffy and the sugar is fully dissolved into the butter, about 5 minutes. Beat in the soft cream cheese about 45 grams (3 tbsp) at a time until fully incorporated. Then add the powdered sugar, lemon zest, lemon juice, vanilla and salt and mix to incorporate. Leave the frosting at room temperature until the cake or cupcakes are fully cooled and you're ready to frost them.

When the cakes are cooled, run a butter knife around the edge of each pan. Remove one, transferring it to a serving plate or cake stand. Top the plated cake round with about 180 milliliters (¾ cup) of the frosting and spread it into an even layer. Top it with the second layer and spread with more frosting. Add the final cake layer and cover the top and sides with the frosting, swooshing as desired. I like to use a small offset spatula for this. For cupcakes, remove them from the tin and place on a platter. Using an offset spatula or butter knife, frost each cupcake in swooshes, creating any patterns you like. If you're comfortable with a pastry bag and piping tip, use that as well on either the cake or cupcakes. Garnish the cake or each cupcake with a little coconut and some chopped walnuts.

Caramelized Grapefruit Brown Sugar Cake

This cake was inspired by a classic caramelized brown sugar–topped broiled grapefruit. I've always loved how the brown sugar works against the bitterness of the citrus, and it was easy to imagine how well it could work as an upside-down cake. It's sweet, sour and tangy, and the honey yogurt topping makes it almost like breakfast. I may or may not have eaten it for breakfast multiple times while testing this recipe. If you're feeling ambitious, you can kiss the finished cake with a blow torch or a few seconds under the broiler for a brûlée effect or enjoy as is with the honey yogurt.

MAKES ONE 9 X 9-INCH (23 X 23-CM) CAKE

Topping

1 large pink or ruby red grapefruit

57 g (4 tbsp) unsalted butter, softened at room temperature

73 g (½ cup) dark brown sugar, packed

Cake

114 g (1 stick) unsalted butter, softened at room temperature

Zest from ½ of the grapefruit, about 2 tsp

250 g (1¼ cups) granulated sugar

2 large eggs

1 tsp vanilla extract

110 g (½ cup) active sourdough starter

188 g (1½ cups) all-purpose flour

1 tsp kosher salt

1 tsp baking powder

¼ tsp baking soda

60 ml (¼ cup) plain Greek-style yogurt

Heat the oven to 350°F (177°C) with a rack in the center. Line a 9 x 9–inch (23 x 23–cm) square cake pan with a rectangle of parchment paper, allowing for a 2-inch (5-cm) overhang on two opposite sides. Spray liberally with neutral nonstick cooking spray. Set aside.

To make the topping: First zest half the grapefruit into a large mixing bowl. Set aside. Using a large knife, trim the top and bottom off the grapefruit so it sits securely on a cutting board. Run the knife down the side of the fruit to remove the peel in segments, removing as much of the white pith as possible. Turn the grapefruit on its side and slice into ½-inch (1-cm)-thick rounds. You should get eight to nine slices. Set aside.

In a small pot over medium heat, melt the butter. Add the dark brown sugar and cook, stirring constantly, until all the sugar has dissolved into the butter and the mixture is smooth and bubbling, about 2 minutes. Remove it from the heat and quickly drizzle it into the bottom of the prepared cake pan. It cools quickly so you'll want to work fast; don't worry if it's not in a perfectly even layer, as it will spread and even out during baking. Layer the slices of grapefruit on top however you like, letting them overlap if needed.

To make the cake: Combine the butter with the grapefruit zest and granulated sugar in a large mixing bowl. Beat it together using a wooden spoon or hand beaters, until light and fluffy. Add the eggs and vanilla. Mix to combine. Add the sourdough starter and mix just until uniform. Switch to a spatula and add the flour, salt, baking powder and baking soda, folding until uniform and no dry bits remain. Fold through the yogurt until evenly distributed.

(continued)

Caramelized Grapefruit Brown Sugar Cake
(Continued)

Honey Yogurt

120 ml (½ cup) plain Greek-style yogurt

15 ml (1 tbsp) honey

Transfer the batter to the cake pan, using the spatula to smooth it over the grapefruit slices in an even layer. Bake until set and a toothpick or cake tester comes out clean, 35 to 40 minutes.

While the cake bakes, make the honey yogurt: Add the yogurt and honey to a small bowl and mix to combine. Transfer to the fridge until serving.

When the cake is done, remove it from the oven and let it cool in the pan for 5 minutes. Run a butter knife around the edge to loosen it from the sides of the pan. Place a serving plate on top of the pan, and using potholders or a dry towel, quickly invert the cake onto the plate, tapping it gently on your work surface if needed. Gently remove the pan and peel away the parchment paper. If you're so inclined, gently torch the grapefruit slices with a culinary blowtorch, or carefully pop it under the broiler for a few seconds—make sure it's on an oven-safe platter. Let the cake cool for 10 minutes before slicing and serving with the honey yogurt either dolloped on top or on the side.

Milk Chocolate–Caramel Gâteau Breton

MAKES ONE 10-INCH (25-CM) GÂTEAU

A Gâteau Breton is impressive because it's filled. And any filled pastry or dessert always makes people think you really know what you're doing. But it's actually silly easy and you can casually whip one up for a satisfying cross between a torte and a shortbread, with my funky little sourdough twist that makes it extra flaky on top. You want the caramel chocolate ganache to be a thick, spreadable consistency, which is best achieved by letting it sit at room temperature for several hours or even overnight, so plan to make it ahead. It's also imperative that you allow the gâteau to cool fully before slicing. Even consider making it the day before you want to serve and let it sit at room temperature. If not fully cooled, you'll get a pool of ganache flooding all over the place when you slice it. Worse things have happened, I'm sure, but you want a nicely set filling for a perfect, clean slice.

Filling

170 g (6 oz) good-quality milk chocolate, chopped

177 ml (¾ cup) heavy cream

84 g (6 tbsp) unsalted butter, room temperature

150 g (¾ cup) granulated sugar

187 ml (¾ cup) water

¾ tsp kosher salt

Make the filling at least 8 hours and up to a day ahead of time. Place the chopped chocolate in a deep bowl and set aside. In a small saucepan, about 1-quart (1-L) capacity, bring the cream just to a boil, about 5 minutes. As soon as it starts to bubble, remove from the heat and add the butter to melt. Set aside. In another small saucepan, combine the sugar with the water. It should be the texture of wet sand, with no sugar crystals remaining on the sides of the pot. Over high heat, cook the sugar to a whiskey-colored caramel, 10 to 12 minutes. If you're new to caramel, you can use a candy thermometer. Watch it closely as once the sugar is fully dissolved, it will turn from clear syrup to caramel quickly. Do not stir the sugar and water until you see it start to change color, as this can cause crystallization.

When you see the first signs of caramelization, carefully swirl the syrup around in the pan a few times so it colors evenly. Once it takes on a honey hue and reads 355 to 360°F (179 to 182°C) on a thermometer, reduce the heat to low and carefully drizzle in the cream and butter mixture. The mixture will bubble up significantly, so do this slowly, a little bit at a time, letting the mixture settle before adding more. Stir the caramel gently until the mixture is uniform, and let it simmer for 1 minute. Remove from the heat and pour it over the chocolate. Allow it to sit for 5 minutes, then stir with a spatula until the mixture comes together in a smooth ganache. Add the salt and stir to fully dissolve and combine. Cover and leave the ganache to sit at room temperature until it thickens and is a spreadable, soft butter-like consistency, at least 8 hours and ideally overnight.

(continued)

Milk Chocolate-Caramel Gâteau Breton (Continued)

Gâteau

281 g (2¼ cups) all-purpose flour, plus more as needed

228 g (2 sticks) unsalted butter, softened at room temperature

150 g plus 13 g (¾ cup plus 1 tbsp) granulated sugar, divided

1 tsp kosher salt

73 g (⅓ cup) active sourdough starter

4 large egg yolks

Seeds of 1 vanilla bean

1 large egg white

1 tsp water

To make gâteau: In a food processor, combine the flour, butter, 150 grams (¾ cup) of sugar and salt. Pulse until crumbly. Add the sourdough starter, egg yolks and vanilla seeds. Pulse until just combined but still crumbly.

Divide the dough into two equal portions, shaping each one into a disc about 6 inches (15 cm) in diameter, and wrap them in plastic. You can dust your hands with a little flour if it's sticky. Chill the dough for at least 2 hours.

When you're ready to bake, heat the oven to 350°F (177°C) with a rack in the center. Lightly spray a deep 10-inch (25-cm) fluted tart pan with a removable bottom, with a neutral nonstick cooking spray. Set aside. Place a large sheet of parchment paper on your work surface, dust it liberally with flour and place the first disc of dough on top, rolling it out to about 11 inches (28 cm) in diameter. If the dough cracks a bit, don't worry, it's very forgiving and you can patch it up as you go.

Gently transfer the disc of dough to the tart pan. I like to do this by placing the removable bottom on top of the dough and then sliding my hand underneath the bottom parchment. Then, carefully and quickly, invert it into the fluted ring. Do not worry if the dough cracks or breaks a little; it's delicate but very forgiving. Settle it into the pan and gently press it in, patching up any areas as needed and allowing any excess dough to fall over the top edge and trim away.

(continued)

Milk Chocolate-Caramel Gâteau Breton (Continued)

Fill the shaped dough with the caramel chocolate ganache, smoothing into an even layer. Roll out the second disc of dough in the same manner and place it on top of the chocolate filling.

Seal the edge of the gâteau by pressing the top round of dough down with your thumbs around the edges, pinching off any excess dough as you go, and sealing the filling inside.

Mix the egg white with the water and brush it across the top of the gâteau using your fingers or a pastry brush. Then dust the top of the tart with 13 grams (1 tbsp) of granulated sugar and place it on a sheet pan to catch any potential leaks. Transfer it to the oven and bake until the gâteau is a deep golden brown, 40 to 45 minutes.

Remove from the oven and allow the gâteau to cool completely in the pan, at least 4 hours and ideally overnight, so the ganache filling can fully set. If sliced too soon, the filling will spill out. When cool, gently remove the outer ring. Place on a platter to slice and enjoy.

Tangerine Dream Cake

MAKES ONE 10-INCH (25-CM) CAKE

5 small tangerines

300 g (1½ cups) granulated sugar, divided

120 ml (½ cup) water

114 g (1 stick) unsalted butter, softened at room temperature

110 g (½ cup) active sourdough starter

2 large eggs

1 tsp vanilla extract

188 g (1½ cups) all-purpose flour

70 g (¾ cup) sweetened, shredded coconut flakes

1 tsp baking powder

1 tsp kosher salt

¼ tsp baking soda

60 ml (¼ cup) buttermilk

My neighbor ordered a case of tangerines during the peak of the pandemic, and she shared some with me. It was a gloomy spring day, so I whipped up this bright cake, sharing it with the same neighbor. I snacked on the rest myself here and there, and the fruit and caramel kept it moist for several days. "Tangerine Dream" conveniently has a ring to it, but I called it that because I remember that week being particularly awful. The success of this cake lifted my spirits, made me hopeful and was transportive when I needed it the most. I hope it gives you all the same feels.

Heat the oven to 325ºF (165ºC) with a rack in the center. Line a 10-inch (25-cm) round cake pan with a circle of parchment paper and spray well with neutral nonstick cooking spray. Set the pan aside. Zest the tangerines into a large mixing bowl and set aside. Using a paring knife, trim off the top and bottom of each tangerine so it sits securely on your cutting board. Run the knife down the sides of each tangerine to remove the peel and pith, leaving as much of the flesh as possible. Turn each tangerine on its side and slice into rounds, about four to five slices per piece of fruit. Pick out and discard any seeds. Arrange the slices in the prepared cake pan, covering the bottom and overlapping if needed.

In a small saucepan, combine 100 grams (½ cup) of sugar with the water. It should be the texture of wet sand, with no sugar crystals remaining on the sides of the pot. Over high heat, cook the sugar to a light, honey-colored caramel, about 8 minutes. If you're new to caramel, you can use a candy thermometer. Watch it closely as once the sugar is fully dissolved, it will turn from clear syrup to caramel quickly. Do not stir the sugar and water until you see it start to change color, as I find this can cause crystallization.

When you see the first signs of caramelization, carefully swirl the syrup around in the pan a few times so it colors evenly. Once it takes on a light honey hue and reads 340 to 350ºF (171 to 177ºC) on a thermometer, carefully but quickly pour the caramel over the tangerine segments. Don't worry if it doesn't cover the whole surface of the pan; it'll distribute as it bakes. Set aside.

To the mixing bowl with the zest, add the butter and remaining sugar. Cream together with a wooden spoon or hand beaters, until light and fluffy. Add the sourdough starter, eggs and vanilla and mix well. Add the flour, coconut, baking powder, salt and baking soda and fold together with a spatula until just uniform. Fold the buttermilk through.

(continued)

Tangerine Dream Cake (Continued)

Transfer the batter to the pan, spreading over the segments into an even layer. Bake until golden and set and a toothpick or cake tester comes out clean, 35 to 40 minutes.

Allow to cool in the pan for 5 minutes, then run a knife around the edge of the cake and, with oven mitts or a towel, invert onto a platter or cutting board, tapping it gently to release the cake. Do this while it's still hot so the caramel doesn't set, causing the cake to stick to the pan. Peel away the parchment circle and discard, allowing the cake to cool completely before slicing and serving.

Apricot, Chèvre, Rye and Almond Upside-Down Cake

MAKES ONE 8-INCH (20-CM) CAKE

Cake

114 g (1 stick) unsalted butter, softened at room temperature, divided

200 g plus 26 g (1 cup plus 2 tbsp) granulated sugar, divided

6 fresh ripe apricots, halved and pitted

27 g (¼ cup) sliced almonds

113 g (4 oz) fresh chèvre, softened at room temperature

½ tsp vanilla extract

2 large eggs

110 g (½ cup) active sourdough starter

63 g (½ cup) all-purpose flour

30 g (¼ cup) rye flour

½ tsp kosher salt

½ tsp baking powder

¼ tsp baking soda

This cake has a very restrained sweetness, and a little funkiness thanks to fresh chèvre (goat cheese) and sourdough. It all happened out of necessity one day, when I was out of the cream cheese a recipe I was making called for but found a log of chèvre in the fridge. I swapped it in, made a few little adjustments, and the rest is history. It's a home run with the sourdough, and apricots are downright lovely here, especially with a little rye flour and almonds in the mix. Since the chèvre has a lower water content than cream cheese, the honey syrup adds moisture and a little extra sweetness to the finished cake.

To make the cake: Heat oven to 325°F (165°C) with a rack in the middle. Butter a deep 8-inch (20-cm) cake pan with 14 grams (1 tbsp) of butter and dust with 26 grams (2 tbsp) of sugar, fully coating the inside then tapping out any excess.

Place the cut apricots in the pan, alternating flesh side down, creating a circle with two halves in the center. Distribute the almonds evenly over and in the spaces between the apricots.

In a large mixing bowl, use a wooden spoon or hand beaters to cream together the remaining 100 grams (7 tbsp) of butter with the chèvre. Add the remaining 200 grams (1 cup) of sugar and mix vigorously until fluffy. Add the vanilla and the eggs, one at a time, mixing to fully incorporate. Add the sourdough starter and mix until uniform. Gently fold in the all-purpose flour, rye flour, salt, baking powder and baking soda. Mix until no dry bits remain.

Transfer the batter to the cake pan, using the spatula to spread it into an even layer over the apricots. Bake until set and golden brown on top and a toothpick or cake tester comes out clean, 40 to 45 minutes.

(continued)

Apricot, Chèvre, Rye and Almond Upside-Down Cake (Continued)

Syrup

30 ml (2 tbsp) honey

15 ml (1 tbsp) water

Remove the cake from the oven and allow it to cool for 5 minutes. Then, run a butter knife around the edge of the pan to release the cake from the sides and place a platter on top of the pan. With oven mitts or a towel, invert onto a platter, tapping it gently to release the cake. Do this while it's still hot so the sugar doesn't set, causing the cake to stick to the pan.

While the cake cools, make the honey syrup: In a small saucepan over low heat, dissolve the honey with the water, until it starts to bubble. Simmer for 1 minute. Remove from the heat and brush the syrup all over the cake with a pastry brush. This can be done while the cake is still warm or once it has fully cooled to room temperature. Serve warm or at room temperature.

Raspberry-Coconut Cake with Lime Glaze

I've had a bit of a love affair with coconut cake over the past decade and find myself reimagining it often, on various menus and with the seasons. Coconut paired with lime is one of my standards, but when I converted it to include sourdough, I felt like it needed one extra, bright fruit component to balance it all out. I love how fresh raspberries tie-dye the inside of this cake, make it impossibly moist and provide pucker-inducing pops of acidity. The glaze makes it even more of a treat.

MAKES ONE 10-INCH (25-CM) CAKE

Heat the oven to 325°F (165°C) with a rack in the center. Line a 10-inch (25-cm) round cake pan with a circle of parchment paper and spray well with neutral nonstick cooking spray. Set aside.

Cake

250 g (1¼ cups) granulated sugar

114 g (1 stick) unsalted butter, room temperature

110 g (½ cup) active sourdough starter

2 large eggs

1 tsp vanilla extract

Zest of 1 lime

156 g (1¼ cups) all-purpose flour

62 g (⅔ cup) shredded, sweetened coconut flakes

1 tsp kosher salt

1 tsp baking powder

¼ tsp baking soda

60 ml (¼ cup) buttermilk

246 g (1 pint) fresh raspberries

To make the cake: In a mixing bowl, cream together the sugar and butter until light and fluffy with hand beaters or a wooden spoon. Add the sourdough starter, eggs, vanilla and lime zest and mix gently to fully incorporate. The mixture may look a little broken at this point, but don't worry. Add the flour, coconut, salt, baking powder and baking soda and fold together until no dry patches remain. Add the buttermilk, folding it gently through. Add the raspberries and fold together to evenly distribute them in the batter. Transfer the batter to the prepared pan, smoothing it out into an even layer.

Bake until golden and a toothpick or cake tester comes out clean, about 40 minutes. Remove the cake from the oven and allow it to cool completely in its pan.

(continued)

Raspberry-Coconut Cake with Lime Glaze (Continued)

Glaze

170 g (1⅓ cups) powdered sugar

45 ml (3 tbsp) lime juice

Zest of 1 lime

Pinch of kosher salt

Water, milk or buttermilk, as needed

Garnish (optional)

12 g (2 tbsp) shredded, sweetened coconut flakes

Handful of fresh raspberries

To make the glaze: In a small bowl, combine the powdered sugar, lime juice, zest and salt. Mix with a spoon or small spatula until smooth. It should be thick, yet pourable. If it's too thick, add a little water, milk or buttermilk, 1 teaspoon at a time, until it's to your liking.

When the cake is fully cooled, run a knife around the edge of the pan to release it from the sides. Gently remove the cake from the pan and transfer it to a serving platter. Top with the glaze, pouring in the center of the cake and letting it spread to the edges, using a spatula to coax it into place. Garnish with the coconut and more raspberries, if using. Allow the glaze to set for 30 minutes before slicing.

Olive Oil, Cherry and Almond Torte

MAKES ONE 10-INCH (25-CM) TORTE

This recipe started as something completely different. I originally made it with peaches. I tested it, and it worked. I liked it, and then I moved on. I sent it off, with dozens of others, to my recipe tester, Chloe, to get a second set of eyes, do some editing and just work out some minor kinks. One day she texted me and said, "Can I talk to you about the olive oil peach torte?" "Sure," I said. "It's nice. I like it, but it's not a love match. Can I work on it for you?" She ran with it and came back about a week later with this cherry version we both decided was truly special. Chloe is one of the many talented people to help this book come to life, and it's nothing short of an honor to have her creative contribution to this book in the form of this sweet torte.

Torte

200 g plus 5 g (1 cup plus 1 tsp) granulated sugar, divided

120 ml (½ cup) olive oil

2 large eggs

1 tsp almond extract

55 g (¼ cup) active sourdough starter

125 g (1 cup) all-purpose flour

75 g (½ cup) fine cornmeal

1 tsp kosher salt

½ tsp baking powder

150 g (1 cup) pitted cherries, fresh or thawed from frozen

30 g (¼ cup) sliced almonds

Honey Cream

240 ml (1 cup) heavy cream

15 ml (1 tbsp) honey

Pinch of kosher salt

Heat the oven to 350°F (177°C) with a rack in the center. Spray a 10-inch (25-cm) round springform pan with neutral nonstick cooking spray and set aside.

To make the torte: In a large mixing bowl, combine the 200 grams (1 cup) sugar and the olive oil. Using a hand blender on high speed, beat until it's light in color and thickened, 3 to 4 minutes. Alternatively, you can do this in a stand mixer with a paddle attachment or by hand, whisking vigorously. Add the eggs and almond extract and mix to combine. Gently mix in the sourdough starter until uniform.

In another mixing bowl, combine the all-purpose flour, cornmeal, salt and baking powder, whisking to combine. Using a spatula, fold the dry into the wet ingredients until no dry patches remain. Transfer the batter to the prepared pan, using the spatula to smooth it out into an even layer. Arrange the cherries on top, without pressing them into the batter. Sprinkle with the almonds and remaining 1 teaspoon granulated sugar and transfer to the oven. Bake until the edges are golden brown and slightly pulling away from the edges of the pan, 40 to 45 minutes. Remove from the oven and allow to cool to room temperature before removing the outer ring of the pan.

While the torte cools, make the honey cream: In a mixing bowl, whip the cream to soft peaks using a whisk or hand beaters. Add the honey and salt. Whip for 1 minute, or until stiff peaks form. Keep refrigerated until serving and dollop alongside slices of the torte.